New Directions for
Community Colleges

Arthur M. Cohen
EDITOR-IN-CHIEF

Florence B. Brawer
ASSOCIATE EDITOR

Carrie B. Kisker
MANAGING EDITOR

From Distance Education to E-Learning:
Lessons Along the Way

Beverly L. Bower
Kimberly P. Hardy
EDITORS

Number 128 • Winter 2004
Jossey-Bass
San Francisco

FROM DISTANCE EDUCATION TO E-LEARNING: LESSONS ALONG THE WAY
Beverly L. Bower, Kimberly P. Hardy (eds.)
New Directions for Community Colleges, no. 128

Arthur M. Cohen, Editor-in-Chief
Florence B. Brawer, Associate Editor

NEW DIRECTIONS FOR COMMUNITY COLLEGES (ISSN 0194-3081, electronic ISSN 1536-0733) is part of The Jossey-Bass Higher and Adult Education Series and is published quarterly by Wiley Subscription Services, Inc., A Wiley Company, at Jossey-Bass, 989 Market Street, San Francisco, California 94103-1741. Periodicals Postage Paid at San Francisco, California, and at additional mailing offices. POSTMASTER: Send address changes to New Directions for Community Colleges, Jossey-Bass, 989 Market Street, San Francisco, California 94103-1741.

SUBSCRIPTIONS cost $80.00 for individuals and $170.00 for institutions, agencies, and libraries. Prices subject to change. See order form in back of book.

EDITORIAL CORRESPONDENCE should be sent to the Editor-in-Chief, Arthur M. Cohen, at the Graduate School of Education and Information Studies, University of California, Box 951521, Los Angeles, California 90095-1521. All manuscripts receive anonymous reviews by external referees.

New Directions for Community Colleges is indexed in Current Index to Journals in Education (ERIC).

Microfilm copies of issues and articles are available in 16mm and 35mm, as well as microfiche in 105mm, through University Microfilms Inc., 300 North Zeeb Road, Ann Arbor, Michigan 48106-1346.

CONTENTS

EDITORS' NOTES   1
Beverly L. Bower, Kimberly P. Hardy

1. From Correspondence to Cyberspace: Changes and   5
Challenges in Distance Education
Beverly L. Bower, Kimberly P. Hardy
Distance education has an extensive history, both nationally and internationally, with roots tracing back over 150 years. This chapter discusses the profound impact this learning method has had on higher education and the role community colleges have played in its proliferation, with a specific focus on Web-based education.

2. Twelve Maxims for Creating and Sustaining a Successful   13
E-Learning Enterprise
James Olliver
This chapter discusses twelve necessary maxims for an institution to launch and sustain a distance education program successfully. Specific examples are based on the experiences of faculty and administrators at St. Petersburg College in Florida.

3. Institutional Issues When Distance Learning Joins the   23
Mainstream
Steven G. Sachs
The Extended Learning Institute at Northern Virginia Community College is a collegewide unit in a multicampus environment. This chapter examines the challenges involved in moving distance learning into the institutional mainstream, including administrative, organizational, political, and decision-making issues.

4. Access and Technology   31
Lemuel W. Watson
This chapter explores the issues and challenges that community colleges face in bringing technology to the masses and makes suggestions to guide colleges in improving access to technology.

5. Five Important Lessons About the Cost of E-Learning   39
Carol Scarafiotti
Rio Salado College in Arizona has developed strategies to contain and reduce costs while improving learning through electronic technology. The author makes recommendations for cost containment that may prove helpful to community colleges looking to reduce expenses associated with distance learning programs.

6. Instructional and Work Life Issues for Distance Learning   47
Faculty
Kimberly P. Hardy, Beverly L. Bower
As community college faculty become more involved with online
courses, questions emerge regarding intellectual property, workload,
instructional techniques, and faculty role. These issues must be examined in the context of the online environment rather than the traditional classroom if instructional expectations are to be fulfilled.

7. New Roles for Student Support Services in Distance Learning   55
Deborah L. Floyd, Deborah Casey-Powell
Distance learners require institutional support beyond the electronic
classroom. Community colleges can strengthen their online programs
by ensuring that student support services, including admissions, advising, career and counseling services, registration, financial aid, and
library services, meet the needs of both distance learners and students
enrolled in on-campus courses.

8. Oregon's Seventeen-Member Statewide Distance Learning   65
Collaborative
Cynthia R. Andrews
The Oregon Community Colleges Distance Learning Consortium was
initiated to meet the difficulties community colleges face in delivering
online education. This chapter describes the challenges and successes
Oregon's collaborative has experienced in addressing issues of shared
curriculum, course delivery mechanisms, and support infrastructure.

9. Meeting the Next Phase of Challenges   73
Lenoar Foster
This chapter acknowledges the challenges of a constantly evolving technology and describes innovative approaches to teaching, learning, and
partnerships that will be essential to the next phase of technological
implementation.

10. Policy: The Inconspicuous Barrier to Expanding E-Learning   79
in Community Colleges
Bruce N. Chaloux
The rapid growth of e-learning throughout the country has produced a
number of policy issues that have yet to be resolved. The Southern
Regional Education Board's Distance Learning Policy Laboratory identifies and discusses barriers to the growth and development of e-
learning in community colleges, including fiscal policy, faculty roles
and responsibilities, intellectual property, outsourcing, student services,
credit transfer and articulation, and financial aid issues.

11. Sources and Information for Distance Educators   85
Veronica Diaz
This chapter provides information and resources on issues of interest
to community college distance educators, including the Americans with
Disabilities Act, the TEACH Act, and the creation, sharing, and use of
learning objects.

INDEX   93

EDITORS' NOTES

Correspondence, telecourses, e-learning: distance education has undergone many changes over the years, and community colleges, the postsecondary institutions most open to change, have adapted at every step. Indeed, the technological landscape has evolved significantly since 1997, when the *New Directions for Community Colleges* series last published an issue on distance education. Even the terminology used in describing this phenomenon has changed. What was then universally called distance education is known today as *distance learning* (which emphasizes student learning), *distributed learning* (which focuses on the connection between traditional and off-campus delivery), and *e-learning* (which refers to education delivered electronically).

In creating distance education opportunities, community colleges are responding to the mounting demands of nontraditional students, working professionals, and lifelong learners. They are also trying to compete successfully with various educational providers and answer to public and legislative calls for cost effectiveness and reform. However, several organizational and systematic barriers, such as cost, resistance to change, and questions about quality, challenge the growth of distance education. Community college educators and policymakers who are committed to distance education must find ways of addressing these issues if community colleges are going to inhabit a significant position in our knowledge-based society.

Even though distance education has become the growth industry of higher education, and technological advances continue to improve and expand online educational opportunities, many community colleges struggle to maintain innovation in distance education efforts. Throughout this volume, authors point out ways that community college educators and policymakers can and have incorporated good practices for successful, quality distance education efforts.

Chapter One, by Beverly Bower and Kimberly Hardy, presents a historical overview of distance education. This chapter illustrates how distance education has evolved into today's e-learning, and introduces some of the challenging problems that will arise as distance education continues to evolve. This chapter sets the stage for the issues and evidence of success that will be presented in the rest of the volume.

In Chapter Two, James Olliver draws on the experiences of St. Petersburg College and Project Eagle to demonstrate ways in which community colleges can create and sustain successful distance learning initiatives. Laying out twelve maxims for success, Olliver explains how distance education affects and changes an organization, and discusses how these changes should be handled to achieve the best results.

Steven Sachs takes the discussion of organizational change further in Chapter Three, as he describes the maturing of the distance education enterprise at Northern Virginia Community College. Sachs's chapter signals that the work of maintaining vibrant, innovative distance learning programs does not end when the newness wears off; rather, these programs will be challenged to maintain momentum when they become part of the mainstream organization.

Whether the programs are new or mature, providing access to the tools necessary to participate in the latest forms of distance education is an issue for many community colleges. Like community colleges in general, distance education aims to increase student access to educational opportunities, yet the growing reliance on electronic delivery may actually reduce access for disadvantaged student populations. Chapter Four, written by Lemuel Watson, addresses the social and economic factors that may limit access to technology, and the difficult questions that must be asked if community colleges are to provide broad access.

Early administrative proponents of distance learning hoped that technology would not only help institutions increase access but also reduce educational delivery costs through economies of scale and reduced need for campus facilities. As the marketplace expanded, however, so did the competition and the technology, and community colleges realized that creating the quality courses and environments needed to attract and retain distance learners did not produce the magnitude of savings they had originally expected. In Chapter Five, Carol Scarafiotti discusses five lessons Rio Salado College learned about the costs of e-learning.

In addition to managing costs, educators seeking to produce quality programs must also address the impact of distance education on faculty work life. In Chapter Six, Kimberly Hardy and Beverly Bower address issues of importance to community college distance learning faculty. In particular, they discuss how involvement in distance education affects workload and changes the instructor's role.

As important as faculty are to distance education efforts, students, in the end, are the most important constituents; without student success, distance education is pointless. In Chapter Seven, Deborah Floyd and Deborah Casey-Powell describe a model for designing student support services to assist both distance and on-campus students. This five-component model addresses support services from the learner's—rather than the institution's—point of view.

Because of the complex challenges presented by distance education and growing competition in the marketplace, an increasing number of institutions view collaborative arrangements or consortiums as effective ways to support distance learning. In Chapter Eight, Cynthia Andrews describes the challenges and successes Oregon's community colleges experienced in creating a statewide distance learning collaborative.

Consortiums such as Oregon's seventeen-member distance learning collaborative may also help address issues such as campus climate, access, and faculty roles in the online environment. Chapter Nine, by Lenoar Foster, discusses these issues in detail, and predicts the next phase in distance education. The chapter then provides promising institutional strategies for meeting the inherent challenges as distance learning continues to evolve.

Drawing from his work with the Southern Regional Education Board, Bruce Chaloux examines some of the structural barriers that inhibit the success of distance learning efforts in Chapter Ten. In particular, he addresses the inconspicuous barriers to the growth of e-learning: state and federal financial policies, as well as institutional policies in the areas of tuition, transfer, and student support services.

Concluding this volume, Veronica Diaz offers key resources and information about distance education in Chapter Eleven, and she elaborates on additional topics important to the understanding and advancement of e-learning. Taken together, these chapters illustrate the continuing evolution of distance education in the community college, and describe ways in which community colleges can successfully meet the challenges.

Although this sourcebook covers a variety of important distance learning issues, its scope is not comprehensive. Some topics, such as copyright and the Americans with Disabilities Act, are only briefly discussed, yet they merit attention commensurate with the significant role they play in shaping the distance learning landscape. Our space was limited, and choices were made to include topics we felt had the broadest appeal for *NDCC* series readers.

This is a dynamic time for distance education in community colleges. It is our hope that this volume will provide community college educators and practitioners with a useful understanding of how community colleges are addressing the ever-changing landscape of distance learning to provide quality educational experiences for future distance learners.

Beverly L. Bower
Kimberly P. Hardy
Editors

BEVERLY L. BOWER *is associate professor of higher education at Florida State University and a former community college administrator. She has taught using several distance education platforms and researches teaching and learning in distance education.*

KIMBERLY P. HARDY *is a consultant for MGT of America, Inc., a national higher education research firm. She is a former community college administrator and has worked with the Florida Distance Learning Consortium.*

1

Higher education has provided students with distance learning opportunities for over 150 years. This chapter traces the evolution of distance learning and provides an overview of some of the challenges inherent in learning in an online environment.

From Correspondence to Cyberspace: Changes and Challenges in Distance Education

Beverly L. Bower, Kimberly P. Hardy

After tucking her youngest son in for the night, Carole sits down with her laptop to search the Internet for documents to share with the online discussion group for her class, Introduction to Management. As she browses a PDF file on current business trends, she is reminded of her mother. After Carole and her brothers were in bed, her mother would watch the tapes she brought home from the community college, stopping the machine frequently to take notes. Carole was so proud when her mother received an associate degree in dental hygiene. Although Carole already has her associate degree in legal assisting, she is taking distance education courses in business to advance at her job. Her mother's videotapes and workbooks have been replaced by a computer that enables Carole to access vast amounts of information and work with other distance education students. Noting the changes over the years, Carole wonders, "What will distance education be like when my children are ready for college?"

The United States Distance Learning Association (n.d.) defines distance education as the "acquisition of knowledge and skills through mediated information and instruction, encompassing all technologies and other forms of learning at a distance" (n.p.). Though there are a variety of definitions of distance education, this particular one encompasses the various facets of this learning environment. And unlike the many definitions that

NEW DIRECTIONS FOR COMMUNITY COLLEGES, no. 128, Winter 2004 © Wiley Periodicals, Inc.

address only current forms of distance learning (for example those associated with electronic technology), this definition encompasses distance education's long history.

This chapter presents a brief history of distance education, from correspondence courses to today's lessons in cyberspace. In addition, the chapter examines the characteristics of community colleges that foster the growth of distance learning and provides an overview of the expectations and challenges as distance education moves into the mainstream of postsecondary education.

A Brief History of Distance Education

Until the twentieth century, print was the only medium available for distance education. Correspondence study, a method of learning via postal mail, was the first form of distance education. The earliest record of this type of educational opportunity comes from an advertisement in the *Boston Gazette* on March 20, 1728, in which a shorthand teacher by the name of Caleb Phillipps offered to send weekly lessons to prospective students who lived in the country and wished to learn shorthand. However, the first evidence of an established institution of higher education offering distance education came over one hundred years later, in an 1833 advertisement from a Swedish university extending the opportunity to study composition via the post (Holmberg, 2002).

Seven years later, an Englishman named Isaac Pitman adapted his system of shorthand to fit on postcards, which were then mailed to students. The students were instructed to use the shorthand to transcribe Bible selections and to return the transcriptions to Pitman for correction. A few years later the Phonographic Correspondence Society, which later became the Sir Isaac Pitman Correspondence Colleges, was formed to continue his work. Not long after that, in 1856, Charles Toussaint and Gustav Langenscheidt began a correspondence language school in Berlin (Holmberg, 2002).

Correspondence programs spread rapidly at the end of the nineteenth century, particularly in Britain and the United States, where Anna Eliot Ticknor was a pioneer in distance education. A woman of wealth, Ticknor founded the Boston-based Society to Encourage Study at Home in 1873. The society provided housebound women with a modern course of study that they could complete at their own pace, and included over twenty courses in various subject areas (Simonson, Smaldino, Albright, and Zvacek, 2000). Students were guided through the curriculum with the help of well-to-do, educated women "correspondents," including Cary Agassiz, founder of Radcliffe College, and Elizabeth Cleveland, who helped found the Boston Museum of Fine Arts (Bergmann, 2001). The society's personalized instruction included regular correspondence along with guided readings and frequent examinations to assess the effectiveness of instruction.

Among the other early distance education efforts in the United States were programs begun by Illinois Wesleyan College in 1874 and the Correspondence University of Ithaca, New York, in 1883. William Rainey Harper, the first president of the University of Chicago, was also an early distance educator. In the 1880s, while at the Baptist Union Theological Seminary at Morgan Park, Harper developed correspondence courses in Hebrew ("William Rainey Harper," 2003). Well-known as the father of the American junior college, Harper is also considered by some to be the father of American distance education, because he strongly supported this form of education during his Chicago presidency. Thus, the connection between distance education and community or junior colleges dates back over one hundred years.

Also in the late nineteenth century, a newspaperman named Thomas J. Foster recognized that working adults with ambitions to better themselves needed a convenient way to learn advanced skills. He began developing correspondence courses to help coal miners gain the engineering knowledge they needed to earn promotions to positions such as mine superintendents and foremen. His efforts marked the beginning of the International Correspondence School (ICS) in Scranton, Pennsylvania. ICS enrolled more than a quarter of a million students in its first decade, and by 1894 was offering courses to students in Mexico, America, and Australia (Education Direct, n.d.). Known today as Education Direct, ICS continues to provide a large number of distance education programs via correspondence.

Advances in technology, as well as postal system limitations such as time delays, lost mail, and cost, eventually led to the use of radio transmissions and audio recordings to teach students at a distance. According to Simonson and colleagues, during the 1920s almost two hundred American radio stations delivered distance education to the masses. Audio transmission, however, eventually lessened as a new, visual technology was developed: the television. Although experimentally broadcast in the early 1930s, televised courses were not officially implemented until the 1950s when Western Reserve University became the first U.S. institution to offer a regular series of television courses (Simonson, Smaldino, Albright, and Zvacek, 2000).

Distance education also continued to develop in Britain. In fact, the founding of the British Open University in 1969 can be said to mark the modern movement in distance education. The Open University offered "full degree programs, sophisticated courses, new media and systematic systems evaluation" (Holmberg, 2002, p. 9). The Open University sparked similar programs around the globe, generated public recognition, and conferred prestige on distance education.

The combination of satellite technology introduced in the 1960s and the fiber-optic systems of the late 1980s expanded distance learning options by allowing for two-way live transmission of educational courses (Simonson, Smaldino, Albright, and Zvacek, 2000). These new technologies came with high price tags, because colleges had to establish the networks needed to provide access to students. Advantages such as interactive education, however, have radically changed the face of distance learning and have been well worth the cost of the new technologies.

The Internet is the latest vehicle through which institutions offer credit and noncredit distance courses to students. The Internet has allowed for a variety of asynchronous (two-way communication involving a time delay between transmission and receipt) as well as synchronous (communication without extended time delay) activities, such as chat sessions and online discussions, which can be used to engage learners in student-to-student as well as student-to-instructor interactions.

The Internet also provides access to class materials, the latest research, and current news events. Like previous forms of distance learning, online education allows students to do coursework at times that fit their lives and schedules, rather than conform to a specified class time and location. Finally, this learning environment allows students who would normally not be able to obtain an education because of geographical distance or personal circumstances to do so without physically attending classes.

Distance Education in the Community College

Throughout its history, American higher education has kept up with the nation's social changes by increasing access. The system has evolved from one that primarily served elite and wealthy white adolescent males to one that provides opportunities for a variety of socioeconomically, ethnically, and intellectually diverse groups. Today higher education is not just for traditional college-age students, but also for students who are older, working, and may have families to support. Many of these students cannot afford to quit their jobs to attend school full time. Because of the changing demands of a growing student population, as well as diverse demographics and increased costs, educational institutions have been forced to find ways to become more productive, creative, and flexible in their delivery methods (Baker and Gloster, 1994; Barnard, 1997). The result has been the expansion of distance education in all higher education institutions. Community colleges in particular have responded to these demographic trends, workplace demands, and changing student needs, and have developed innovative ways to provide students with access to higher education.

The community college has traditionally been referred to as *the people's college,* and it is committed to providing access, opportunity, and a full scope of educational options to those who attend. Because of these attributes, as well as the unique populations they serve, community colleges have emerged as leaders in providing distance education, particularly to those students who live in remote areas or have limited access to educational resources (Inman, Kerwin, and Mayes, 1999). The community college commitment to serving students, and its willingness to provide education "anytime, anywhere" makes it a prime candidate to lead distance learning in higher education.

Indeed, some educators feel that the community college is the natural "first tier" with which to begin implementing Web-based instruction systems (Johnstone and Tilson, 1997). According to a recent national study (U.S. Department of Education, 2003), 90 percent of public two-year institutions offered distance education courses in 2000–01. In addition, 95 percent of these institutions used asynchronous Internet technologies as the primary mode of delivery, compared with 87 percent of public four-year institutions. Public two-year institutions accounted for the majority of distance education enrollments in 2000–01 (48 percent of all enrollments were in two-year colleges, compared with 31 percent in public four-year institutions).

Community colleges have also led the nation in applying technology to teaching and learning (Doucette, 1993). There are a number of reasons why they have taken this leadership role. First, community colleges are driven by their distinctive missions, which often emphasize the importance of serving a high number of underprepared students. Technology has assisted community colleges in meeting this challenge effectively. Second, community colleges have also reached out to the workforce and provided opportunities for working adults to attend college on a part- or full-time basis. Distance learning technologies have offered these working adults an opportunity to fulfill their educational goals by allowing them to take courses that are more adaptable to their schedules and to their lives. Third, community colleges have partnered with business and industry to bring the classroom to the workplace, and to customize courses for specific workforce needs. Current distance learning technologies offer new opportunities to provide workplace and workforce education.

As our economy becomes increasingly knowledge-based, there is an ever-greater demand for skilled information technology workers in fields such as manufacturing, health care, and transportation. Because community colleges offer certificate and other programs that can provide entry into information technology jobs, many full- and part-time students are choosing to enter technical education through distance learning programs provided by community colleges. Finally, because community colleges often serve low-income and minority populations, their information technology programs have provided these groups with access to technology and electronic resources and have assisted in bridging the "digital divide"—the gap between technology haves and have-nots (Leach and McPhail, 2003).

Developments in technology have allowed community colleges to provide access for students throughout the nation and the world. As well, given recent state budget shortfalls, many colleges have looked to distance education as a way to save the expense of building new facilities while still accommodating an expanding student population (Bothun, 1997). Although there are certainly costs involved in developing a distance learning network, they can be weighed against the increasing expense of maintaining an infrastructure for on-campus courses. Administrators can choose to build a multi-million-dollar classroom facility or invest the money in building a technological campus infrastructure. For community colleges that are limited in their ability to expand physically, especially those in urban areas, the choice is obvious. Distance education allows them to meet the needs of an ever-changing society and to do so economically and efficiently.

Challenges in Distance Education

Technological advances such as the Internet and its wealth of resources have changed higher education dramatically. These innovations, however, bring new and unfamiliar issues and concerns. In order for community colleges to grow and remain competitive, these challenges must be overcome and educators must be flexible and open to change. Although the following chapters will discuss in more detail some of the complex issues inherent in distance education, the following paragraphs provide an overview of some of the biggest challenges in implementing and sustaining distance education in community colleges.

Not All Stakeholders Will Support Distance Education. In every college, it is likely that one or more stakeholders will argue that distance education is a passing phase and will never replace the traditional classroom. Meanwhile, many more will recognize that this method of learning has irrevocably revolutionized education. Despite these differing opinions, if distance learning is to be a successful method of delivering education, all stakeholders—including faculty, staff, students, and administrators—need to accept it as a practical and effective instructional method. Most new methods of instruction meet with mixed or even negative sentiments, but most gradually come to be accepted as part of standard educational delivery.

Distance Education Requires Changes in Classroom Teaching. Distance education, and Web-based instruction in particular, has changed a number of aspects of teaching, including course content, teaching roles and methods, assessment strategies, interaction, and communication. Research has shown that teaching online requires different skills and pedagogies from those needed in the traditional, face-to-face environment (Fetherston, 2001). Because so many aspects of instruction must be changed when faculty move from the traditional classroom to the distance education environment, it is only natural that many instructors have reservations about this new method of educational delivery.

Distance Education Requires Innovation in Student Support Services. Many accrediting agencies are creating guidelines for the development of community college support systems for e-learners. Library services, financial aid, registration, and advising are just a few of the services that distance learners need access to, preferably without having to physically come to campus. Although many institutions have made concerted efforts to implement these services, many small institutions are unable to afford the changes necessary to meet accreditation requirements and struggle with how to provide the support that distance learners need.

Faculty Must Gain Technological Expertise. Faculty support and training are necessary if distance education is to be successful in community colleges. Administrators have found that they need to help faculty gain technological expertise and instructional design skills. Establishing a marketable presence in the rapidly expanding online education environment requires a team approach to teaching and learning and collaboration between faculty, instructional designers, and programmers. Administrators must provide their faculty and staff with the resources they need to be creative, productive, and more efficient through the use of technology. When adequately implemented, these efforts can result in the development of entirely new departments dedicated to supporting faculty who teach distance education courses.

Distance Education May Change Institutional Culture. Faculty members are not the only individuals whose lives will change as a result of distance education; administrators too must understand the impact that associated technological advances will have on the culture of their institutions. New procedures and policies need to be developed, but faculty, staff, and students also need help in adapting to these changes. It is crucial that community college leaders provide support for distance education programs, because it is impossible to enact change without their support. Community college leaders can help both faculty and staff become comfortable with distance courses and services by providing them with professional development opportunities that address the changes in technology as well as the changes in their roles.

Conclusion

Over the last 150 years, and through a variety of technological advances, distance education has continued to transform higher education. Given the constantly evolving and diverse nature of their student populations, community colleges are the ideal institutions to take the lead in advancing distance education. However, distance education creates technical, pedagogical, and organizational challenges for institutions, and community colleges will need to address faculty, staff, and student expectations and fears. The following chapters will examine how various community colleges and other educational entities have approached these changes and challenges.

References

Baker, W. J., and Gloster, A. S. "Moving Towards the Virtual University: A Vision of Technology in Higher Education." *Cause/Effect,* 1994, *17*(2), 4–11.

Barnard, J. "The World Wide Web and Higher Education: The Promise of Virtual Universities and Online Libraries." *Educational Technology,* 1997, *37*(3), 30–35.

Bergmann, H. F. "The Silent University: The Society to Encourage Studies at Home, 1873–1897." *New England Quarterly,* 2001, 74(3), 447–477.

Bothun, G. D. "Seven Points to Overcome to Make the Virtual University Viable." *Cause/Effect,* 1997, 20(2), 55–65.

Doucette, D. "Transforming Teaching and Learning Using Information Technology: Community College Leadership in Higher Education." *College Board Review,* 1993, 167, 18–26.

Education Direct. "A Tradition of Excellence for Over a Century," n.d. http://www.educationdirect.com/02-our_history.html. Accessed June 26, 2004.

Fetherston, T. "Pedagogical Challenges for the World Wide Web." *Educational Technology Review,* 2001, 9(1). http://dl.aace.org/11556. Accessed Aug. 12, 2004.

Holmberg, B. "The Evolution of the Character and Practice of Distance Education." In L. Foster, B. L. Bower, and L. W. Watson (eds.), *ASHE Reader—Distance Education: Teaching and Learning in Higher Education* (pp. 7–13). Boston: Pearson Custom, 2002.

Inman, E., Kerwin, M., and Mayes, L. "Instructor and Student Attitudes Toward Distance Learning." *Community College Journal of Research and Practice,* 1999, 23(6), 581–591.

Johnstone, S., and Tilson, S. "Implications of a Virtual University for Community Colleges." In C. L. Dillon and R. Citrón (eds.), *Building a Working Policy to Distance Education.* New Directions for Community Colleges, no. 99. San Francisco: Jossey-Bass, 1997.

Leach, E., and McPhail, I. P. "The Community College: On-Ramp to the Cyberhighway." In G. E. de los Santos, A. G. de los Santos, Jr., and M. D. Millron (eds.), *From Digital Divide to Digital Democracy.* Phoenix: League for Innovation in the Community College, 2003.

Simonson, M., Smaldino, S., Albright, M., and Zvacek, S. *Teaching and Learning at a Distance: Foundations of Distance Education.* Upper Saddle River, N.J.: Prentice Hall, 2000.

U.S. Department of Education, National Center for Education Statistics. *Distance Education at Degree-Granting Postsecondary Institutions: 2000–2001* (NCES No. 2003–017). Washington, D.C.: U.S. Department of Education, 2003. http://nces.ed.gov/pubs2003/2003017.pdf. Accessed Aug. 11, 2004.

United States Distance Learning Association. *Distance Learning Glossary,* n.d. http://www.usdla.org/html/resources/dictionary.htm. Accessed Aug. 12, 2004.

"William Rainey Harper." In American Council of Learned Societies (ed.), *Dictionary of American Biography Base Set, 1928–1936.* Farmington Hills, Mich.: Gale Group, 2003.

BEVERLY L. BOWER *is associate professor of higher education at Florida State University and a former community college administrator. She has taught using several distance education platforms and researches teaching and learning in distance education.*

KIMBERLY P. HARDY *is a consultant for MGT of America, Inc., a national higher education research firm. She is a former community college administrator and has worked with the Florida Distance Learning Consortium.*

2

*E-learning programs bring new challenges and
opportunities to community colleges. This chapter
identifies twelve maxims for developing and sustaining a
successful program, and illustrates the ways in which one
community college has applied them.*

Twelve Maxims for Creating and Sustaining a Successful E-Learning Enterprise

James Olliver

Open any journal or educational Web site, and you will likely find some reference to e-learning or distance learning. The demand is growing, the tools for creating and offering distance classes are improving, and the hype is reaching fever pitch. But so are the questions: about accountability, about costs, about outcomes, about competition, and about how e-learning fits into the traditional higher education landscape.

In 1998, St. Petersburg College (SPC) in Florida launched Project Eagle (http://www.spcollege.edu/eagle), a federally funded, multiyear strategic initiative to increase community college students' access to four-year degrees and workforce training through distance education. Although the college experienced its share of setbacks, "aha!" moments, and surprises along the way, it has enjoyed spectacular success in building its eCampus and has come to appreciate that certain fundamental steps must be taken to achieve success. The twelve maxims described in this chapter provide a template for building and sustaining a successful distance learning program. SPC's experiences will serve as a guide for other community colleges working to create and maintain their own distance learning enterprises.

Maxim One: Verify Centrality to Mission

The first maxim, a necessary precondition for all others, is that e-learning must be integral to the institutional mission and have full executive support from the board, the president, and key administrative leaders. If distance

New Directions for Community Colleges, no. 128, Winter 2004   © Wiley Periodicals, Inc.

learning is viewed as secondary to the college's core mission it becomes harder to succeed when tough decisions need to be made.

The first steps to take in implementing an online learning program are including e-learning and a clear direction for its execution in the college mission statement and ensuring support by the leadership. At SPC, two specific references to distance learning were added to a 1998 revision of the mission statement, and e-learning was presented both as a way to enhance access to traditional programs and as an outreach mechanism for specialized areas of expertise.

Howell, Williams, and Lindsay (2003) note that 33 percent of online students are enrolled in for-profit institutions. To compete with these institutions, community colleges must recognize e-learning as central to their mission. Once they do, community college e-learning programs will more easily reach a critical mass of classes, programs, and services. SPC has focused its mission on e-learning and has built a leadership team that understands how to support this mission. As a result, SPC's first online program, in veterinary technology, is now available nationwide.

Maxim Two: Build Institutional Commitment

E-learning is only one of the many good ideas and institutional priorities vying for attention and resources in community colleges. Because it tends to be the "new kid on the block," extra efforts to demonstrate its institution-wide benefits are necessary, and large numbers of faculty and staff should be included in the planning and implementation phases. In addition, e-learning leaders should be deliberate and intentional about sharing the credit and resources gained from online initiatives.

For example, e-learning leaders must show that online and face-to-face instruction can support each other, and that gains made through distance learning can be shared throughout the institution. SPC looks first to existing faculty to teach its online courses, and shares e-learning lab fee revenues with each instructor's home department. As one of the college's provosts stated, "eCampus stands for everyone's campus." Making friends, forging alliances, and navigating institutional politics and processes become extraordinarily important as enrollments in e-learning classes grow.

Maxim Three: Recognize Pedagogical Differences

Just as video cameras were first used to film plays, and ATMs were first used inside banks during normal business hours, e-learning began as the electronic equivalent of a traditional classroom. However, it is no longer acceptable to take existing face-to-face course material, post it on a Web site, and call it an online course. Simply bolting "new technologies onto a fixed plant, a fixed faculty, or a fixed notion of classroom instruction" (Twigg, 2003, p. 28) ignores the pedagogical differences inherent in the e-learning environment and how this difference can affect student outcomes.

The expected outcomes for SPC's online courses are just as high as they are for face-to-face classes; it is only the delivery method that changes. Johnson (2003) notes that "knowledge and skills about effective pedagogy, and when and how to use them" are strong indicators of success in e-learning (p. 149). To be effective, online classes must be planned and organized in advance and crafted with exceptional clarity. Expectations, including the minimum hardware requirements and expected level of student computer skills, must be clearly defined up front. As well, instructors should ensure that content and online communications will be readily accessible to students long before the class even begins.

Successful e-learning instructors must also consider issues in sharing content, either whole courses or learning objects that can be inserted into courses to illustrate or reinforce a concept or lesson. Good online content, including the packaged variety, is ubiquitous on the Net. Through Massachusetts Institute of Technology's Open Courseware Initiative, more than five hundred courses are now freely available (http://ocw.mit.edu/index. html). Textbook manufacturers are also scrambling to provide electronic supplements to their traditional wares to take advantage of the growing e-learning trend, and private companies are providing content-rich packages well beyond the scope of what individual institutions can afford to produce.

Good content is necessary, but it is far from sufficient in providing a good e-learning experience. Equally important is how the content is organized, delivered, and personalized by a dedicated faculty member. Once an online class begins, the role of the faculty member changes from lecturer to navigator and course manager. The professor's primary task becomes facilitating students' learning and motivation, and fostering interaction among students. Clear and constant communication and feedback are necessary, because online learning is passive unless it is organized appropriately and energized by the instructor. Students in online classes can access information quickly, leaving more time "to organize the information in their minds, think, and allow learning to take place. The key is to allow time for processing and provide assignments that encourage and check metacognitive functions throughout the assignments" (Lynch, 2002, p. 12).

Changes in faculty-student interactions are also necessary as conventional office hours give way to virtual office hours, e-mails, and discussion posts. Following in the footsteps of institutions like Athabasca University (http://www.athabascau.ca/misc/expect/index.htm), SPC developed a statement of rights and responsibilities for students, faculty, and staff to address standards for online interactions as well as issues such as academic honesty and online civility.

The tools to achieve pedagogically sound and educationally robust curricula are good and getting even better as learning management systems, software, and student and faculty access to broadband communications expand and mature.

Maxim Four: Invest in Instructional Development and Training

Effective online instruction is fundamentally different from face-to-face instruction, and traditional faculty training does not prepare instructors to navigate this new medium. Community colleges must invest in comprehensive instructional development, redevelopment, and training initiatives. Before teaching online, SPC faculty must take an online course focused on both online pedagogy and the e-learning management system. After completing the course, they are paired with a team of technology-focused curriculum designers and Web design specialists to develop a course based on content and elements of interactivity. Faculty learn basic skills from these technology experts, such as zipping files, creating PDFs, or performing other file management functions. They may also be given an extensive review of the new tools they can use in their courses. For example, SPC's online speech class called for students to present their speeches "live" to other students and the instructor. To fulfill this requirement, students used Click-to-Meet Web conferencing software to present their speeches in real time.

SPC's development team assists faculty in mastering both the pedagogical and the design skills they will need to successfully teach online. The team also counsels instructors in techniques for overcoming the workload inherent in an environment where every student in the class is actively involved. Training is accomplished one-on-one, through targeted workshops and an active online faculty listserv. In addition, SPC offers "cloning" classes—duplications of courses taught by other instructors—and arranges for experienced faculty mentors to guide new faculty the first time they offer an online course.

Maxim Five: Establish a Single Point of Contact

Originally, distance learning at SPC was spread throughout separate departments as early adopters began setting up the Internet equivalent of garage bands for specific programs. Today, however, a single point of contact is essential to address the growing number of student inquiries, program complexities, and standardization of tools and policies required to operate efficiently. For SPC, this has meant the creation and promotion of a central eCampus, with its own identity and staff, to be the gateway to all e-learning curriculum, information, and services.

Key to this "one-stop-shopping" approach is the eCampus Web site, a portal through which all student traffic flows (http://e.spcollege.edu). The site provides electronic access to eCampus staff through e-mail and live chat, and to specialized services such as cyberadvising and "Ask-a-Librarian." A single point of contact provides clarity and efficiency for both the institution and students. However, a centralized eCampus can be a double-edged sword if departments and other institutional entities perceive a rapidly growing online program to be a threat to their autonomy. When community college administrators begin to centralize operations for efficiency, they should communicate with faculty and staff often and in multiple forums to explain and respond to questions, issues, and problems.

Maxim Six: Provide a Full Range of Electronic Services

Musical producer Phil Spector became famous in the 1960s for his "wall of sound," where vocals were surrounded by lush, multilayered instrumentation. This analogy works for successful e-learning programs; students have come to expect a full array of electronic educational services to support and improve on traditional academic and student support services.

These services, such as financial aid and cybertutoring, should be accessible from a distance, but they should also be available on-site for students who prefer that option. For example, a college might stream its awards ceremonies to allow distance learners to attend through interactive videoconference.

At SPC, a "clicks supported by bricks" model is employed: eCampus works closely with the physical campus, and faculty and staff are dedicated both to online and to technologically enhanced face-to-face learning. eCampus staff also coordinate with outlying physical campuses to give online students at each site access to personnel and support services to assist them with their online study. These "wall-of-sound" services are the same ones that face-to-face students currently expect. Thus, providing electronic services for online students may also help a college to attract and retain traditional students.

Maxim Seven: Develop a Robust Technical Infrastructure and Support Network

Imagine offering classes on campus until 10 P.M., only to have the facilities staff turn off the lights at 9 for some "routine maintenance." The equivalent—network interruptions—happens all too often in online classes. E-learning students work at all hours; some have enrolled in distance courses specifically because they could not do the work during conventional hours. Behind the servers and the software there must be an understanding of the nature of online learning and the demands of this different educational method on staffing, hours, and the expertise needed to maintain the system. Increasingly, e-learning requires sophisticated learning management systems and tools. These systems have care-and-feeding requirements that must be fulfilled by staff or outsourced.

Not everyone thrives in an e-learning environment. Meyer (2003) cited evidence that students with certain learning styles and behavioral types are more successful in online classes, as are students who are highly motivated and have good organizational and computer skills. Successful institutions recognize the attributes and differences students bring to the learning environment, and provide them with self-assessment tools. If you believe the popular press, traditional students are coming to college already computer-savvy and equipped, ready to download class materials, view video lectures on their PDAs, and take exams on their cell phones. But most community college students face a variety of scheduling and other life challenges, and those enrolled in online classes face technical challenges as well. Whether the issue is having the necessary e-literacy skills or the right computer and software tools, most students, traditional and non-traditional, still need some assistance in making the transition to an electronic campus.

Institutions must recognize and provide the resources to address these infrastructure and support issues. Some challenges may be handled by the instructor during the courses themselves: by providing clear and detailed instructions about how to access and use tools, creating a rich interactive environment in which to ask questions, or providing a frequently asked questions (FAQ) section. To supplement online resources, institutions frequently provide a "help desk" to answer students' questions and supply them with various self-diagnostic tools. It may be challenging, however, to find the funding and staffing necessary to keep a help desk open for extended hours. Creative approaches like Rio Salado's round-the-clock online tutor service provide useful models (http://www.rio.maricopa.edu/services/student/support/tutoring).

Maxim Eight: Engage in Ongoing Marketing and Market Research

Just as there is a different pedagogy involved in teaching online students, marketing and market research are different in this environment too. A community college's Web site is critical for collecting and providing information to prospective students. SPC also uses strategies to get more exposure on popular search engines, and works with companies and discipline-focused agencies to advertise its e-learning opportunities.

After students visit the eCampus Web site, they should be able to understand the specifics of SPC's operations, programs, and services. Under the heading "Is eCampus right for you?" students can take a model course and thus become familiar with the learning tools they will use if they enroll. Also, front and center on the first page of SPC's Web site is a visitor survey designed to get baseline data on those exploring the site. eCampus also publishes a demographic profile, a student survey of instruction, focus group data, a bimonthly international e-letter on best e-practices, and periodic research briefs. These informational and research initiatives give community college scholars and practitioners a better idea about what is effective and where to improve.

Maxim Nine: Embrace Accountability and an Ongoing Quest for Quality

Questions about the quality of distance learning continue to surface, primarily from those who have not yet experienced it. And, to be fair, there may be quality problems in online classes, just as there are in face-to-face courses. Not getting back to students in a timely fashion in an online course is as unacceptable a practice as using the same lecture notes for twenty years in a face-to-face class. For the foreseeable future, however, the bar will be set higher for the higher-profile online classes.

E-learning programs should study their outcomes and engage in deliberate and ongoing program assessment and enhancement. Students should be given the opportunity to rate online instruction, and changes should be made based on their feedback. Courses should also be reviewed on a regular basis to make sure that information is current, that links work, and that institutionally determined objectives are met. Colleges should also track retention rates, set benchmarks, and monitor grade distributions.

At SPC, online courses are subject to a rigorous review every three years, and the educational technology staff works with departmental faculty to develop and maintain template or model courses that sustain high quality standards. Overall satisfaction with this process is high, and students indicate they are very likely (6.22 on a 7-point scale) to take another online course at the college.

Maxim Ten: Be Realistic About Costs

It is no surprise that fulfilling these maxims requires a significant financial commitment. Although community colleges will incur additional expenses for items like hardware and software, technical support, instructional support, and administrative infrastructure, they will create savings in physical plants and utilities. Many students are also willing to pay an additional fee for online learning, and this can go a long way toward underwriting the additional costs. Interestingly, the increasing infusion of technology into traditional courses, along with the rapid growth of blended classes, means that institutions are investing in some of the items essential for a distance education program even if they do not currently offer significant online options.

A number of models can be used to determine online program costs. For example, the Western Interstate Commission on Higher Education (WICHE) has developed a Technology Costing Methodology (http://www.wcet.info/Projects/tcm/index.asp), and Morgan (2000) created an interactive tool to determine costs (http://thenode.org/networking/july2000/briefs.html). Despite the availability of these tools, community college administrators should be aware that few distance education programs make money.

Maxim Eleven: Do Not Make It More Complicated Than It Really Is

Although the first ten maxims certainly highlight the challenges facing institutions and their e-learning programs, colleges should not succumb to "paralysis by analysis." Because e-learning is new and different, there is an unfortunate tendency to look for new ways of operating when existing systems would work just fine. Take, for example, the issue of academic honesty. An online instructor at SPC confronted a student who had clearly plagiarized in a class assignment. He was surprised that the student was "truly and genuinely clueless" about the need to cite sources. The student's response: "I did the same thing in my face-to-face class last semester and got a B!" Academic honesty is a problem not only in online classes! but across the academy.

Similar issues arise in the area of student evaluations. The same instruments used in traditional classrooms can measure satisfaction in an online course, with a few additional questions to address pedagogical differences. The processes for program review, student appeals, performance standards, and so forth can be adopted or adapted without extensive rework.

Maxim Twelve: Recognize the Rapid Rate of Change in E-Learning

The reality of e-learning is that in the six months between the time this chapter is edited and the date this volume is published, new technologies will be in use at community colleges. Similarly, looking back over SPC's educational e-practices publications from just a year or two ago, much of what were then innovations are now either givens or have been surpassed by other developments. The pace of change, especially in online education, is accelerating at a dizzying rate. Like runners on a treadmill where the speed continuously increases, distance education institutions have to speed up just to stay in place.

Community colleges must also pay attention to the changes in e-learning enrollment. At SPC, the number of online course sections increased from seventy-five to nearly five hundred between the fall of 1999 and the fall of 2003, and student enrollments grew from under twenty-eight hundred to over twelve thousand during the same period. Thus, both staffing and targeted funding were increased to support growth and changes in eCampus operations, and more importantly, to reward and sustain other departments across the institution that support e-learning.

Online learning is a wonderful way for students to take advantage of a community college education, including general education, vocational training, and workforce retraining. But that option requires commitment, resources, and energy, as well as the realization that ongoing improvement and rapid change go with the territory.

Integrating the Twelve Maxims

This chapter outlines how St. Petersburg College has followed the twelve maxims to create and maintain a successful e-learning program. Although each maxim is important on its own, they are also inextricably intertwined and together provide an integrated blueprint for the comprehensive, multi-layered regimen required to develop and sustain a successful program. More information about SPC's experience, including forms, procedures, and best practices, are available on the SPC Project Eagle (http://www.spcollege.edu/eagle) and eCampus (http://e.spcollege.edu) Web sites.

References

Howell, S. L., Williams, P. B., and Lindsay, N. K. "Thirty-Two Trends Affecting Distance Education: An Informed Foundation for Strategic Planning." *Online Journal of Distance Learning Administration,* 6(3), 2003. http://westga.edu/~distance/jmain11.html. Accessed Aug. 12, 2004.

Johnson, J. L. *Distance Education: The Complete Guide to Design, Delivery and Improvement.* New York: Teachers·College Press, 2003.

Lynch, M. M. *The Online Educator: A Guide to Creating the Virtual Classroom.* New York: Routledge Falmer, 2002.

Meyer, K. A. "The Web's Impact on Student Learning." *T.H.E. Journal,* May 2003, pp. 14–24.

Morgan, B. M. "Determining the Costs of Online Courses." *The Node Networking,* July 12, 2000. http://thenode.org/networking/july2000/briefs.html. Accessed Aug. 12, 2004.

Twigg, C. A. "Improving Learning and Reducing Costs: New Models for Online Learning." *EDUCAUSE Review,* Sep.-Oct. 2003, pp. 28–38. http://www.educause.edu/ir/library/pdf/erm0352.pdf. Accessed Aug. 12, 2004.

JAMES OLLIVER is provost for St. Petersburg College's Seminole and eCampuses. He oversees operations on both campuses, supervises the collegewide educational technology and video services departments, and administers the Project Eagle grant.

3

Distance learning began as an institutional innovation, but as the field matures it faces challenges in finding its place in the community college mainstream. This chapter describes the best practices that helped the Extended Learning Institute at Northern Virginia Community College evolve into a mature distance learning program that is successfully integrated into the institution.

Institutional Issues When Distance Learning Joins the Mainstream

Steven G. Sachs

When institutions create distance learning programs, their focus is usually on surviving and building enrollments. They give relatively little thought to the issues the program will face over time as it grows and matures. Which issues will drop away, which will still be important, and which new ones will emerge? This chapter describes some of the original principles that helped Northern Virginia Community College's (NVCC) distance learning program become successful, and some of the new problems it is facing now that it is part of the college mainstream.

NVCC has been offering distance learning courses for almost thirty years. Its distance learning program, the Extended Learning Institute (ELI), was established in 1975 as a collegewide unit in a multicampus environment. Last year over fifteen thousand students enrolled in more than two hundred asynchronous courses; distance learners accounted for 8 percent of the college's enrollment and constituted a student head count that was at times larger than several of the college's traditional campuses. By almost every measure, ELI and distance learning have become very successful. Although that success may have been due in part to luck or fortuitous events, much can be attributed to the foundation on which it was based and how ELI dealt with the challenges it faced.

As an innovative institutional program, ELI was free from a number of administrative, organizational, and political issues. Yet now that it has entered the mainstream of the college, it faces challenges much more complex than when it was a start-up program. How ELI and NVCC respond to these new issues will affect ELI's ability to innovate and respond to new opportunities, and may affect distance learning at the college for years to come. "Mature programs that have been offering distance learning for a long time are caught in the middle between their safe and solid base of experience and the unknown of a new digital world. Whether the new technologies are merely a further enhancement to their programs or a radical paradigm shift remains to be seen" (Sachs, 1999, p. 66).

A Foundation of Best Practices

Northern Virginia Community College's strong foundation of instructional development facilitated ELI's early growth. Among its staff were instructional developers who worked with faculty to design distance learning courses and to create or adapt instructional materials for learners who would not be on campus and would study on their own. ELI's early leaders had experience developing some of the earliest technology-based distance learning programs. During the 1970s and early 1980s, a body of best practices for developing effective instructional units emerged. In 1984, the Division for Instructional Development of the Association for Educational Communications and Technology published a paper pulling these best practices together to describe a model unit that could support "real" innovation (Sachs, 1984). The author of this chapter was also the director of ELI, so it is no surprise that the same best practices would eventually help ELI move into the college mainstream. In the sections that follow I summarize the principles underlying three parts of that model: plans and goals, organization and administration, and decision making. I describe how those principles worked to make ELI successful, and what new issues and challenges have emerged in light of that success.

Plans and Goals. The original model recognized that plans and goals were critical foundations for building a successful program. It recommended comprehensive planning with short- and long-range goals, alternatives for reaching those goals, benchmarks against which to measure accomplishments, and consideration of faculty and institutional readiness for innovation. It also noted the importance of improving instruction rather than encouraging the adoption of any one particular solution (Sachs, 1984).

ELI originally concentrated on developing large courses to quickly maximize distance learning enrollments. Today, as a mature program, ELI's planning and goals are markedly different, often reflecting strategies to manage growth and guide difficult choices about where to spend resources, rather than how to attract new faculty and achieve large-scale growth. Furthermore, tools and technologies once used only in distance learning are now pervasive throughout the college. For example, there are currently more Blackboard course-management system accounts for students in traditional classes than in distance learning courses at ELI. This means that planning and goal setting have become more collaborative and involve greater coordination and negotiation among ELI, traditional academic departments, college information technology staff, and a wide array of support services.

Planning for faculty involvement is also different now that ELI is a mature program. Originally, ELI's faculty was among the most innovative in the college. Their numbers were small and they shared a special bond with each other. Today, with more than eighty faculty, many of whom have been teaching distance learning courses for over a decade, ELI's faculty roster includes both those who are ready for and those resistant to change. There are those who are no longer innovative and who resist any departure from the way things have always been done. At the other end of the spectrum, there are those who are impatient with the pace of implementing new technology now that ELI's size sometimes makes it more difficult to move from one technology to another. This situation is not unique. Terry O'Banion, former executive director of the League for Innovation in the Community College, wrote about the same problem ten years ago: "Sadly, some colleges that were highly innovative in the '60s and '70s have lost that innovative spirit today" (1994, p. 1). ELI's distance learning program is no longer unique as a primary community of innovators; faculty teaching traditional classes use the same instructional tools and wrestle with many of the same student issues. Thus, ELI's planning challenges are now much more similar to those faced by the college as a whole as it tries to keep from growing stale, maintain a strong sense of community among its faculty, and support continued innovation.

Perhaps an even more fundamental change for ELI as a mature program, however, involves choosing appropriate distance learning goals. The importance of this issue cannot be overemphasized, and it comes up again and again in the literature (Compora, 2003; Gross, Gross, and Pirkl, 1998; Levine, Gallagher, Boccuti, and Meyer, 1992; Levy, 2003). Today, planning for distance learning must balance the following goals: using distance learning to solve capacity problems because there are not enough seats in traditional classrooms, increasing distance learning enrollments from outside Northern Virginia to help the college with the state's enrollment-driven funding model, and using distance learning technologies to improve the efficiency of traditional instruction. The choice of goals affects course selection, types of students served, support services required, costs, and even traditional, on-campus class offerings. For ELI, the goal is no longer to grow for growth's sake, and the decisions are no longer ELI's to make alone because each decision has an impact on the rest of the college. This situation is a far cry from the relative independence ELI had in its early years.

Organization and Administration. Although the original model for supporting innovation came after ELI was established in 1975, it identified key organizational and administrative factors that helped ELI ultimately become successful. The model recognized the importance of formal rather than ad hoc status, a full-time staff of well-trained professionals, and administrative independence. It recognized the need for discretionary resources to support innovative projects and for a budget based on hard money. The model also noted the need for formal and informal ties to academic and governance committees to ensure communication and to give faculty a feeling of ownership and connection to the unit (Sachs, 1984).

ELI was created as a separate unit with a high degree of independence, so every decision did not require multiple layers of approval. ELI's director initially reported directly to the president of NVCC. There was a full-time staff and a budget based on the same hard-money formula that supported other college units, so funding was secure and predictable. ELI staff members sat on committees, which helped legitimize distance learning and create important informal and formal communication channels. All of this was consistent with organizational characteristics considered important for success.

These same relationships are still important—even taken for granted. Meanwhile, a new set of issues has emerged over the past several years that challenge many of the assumptions about ELI's relationship with the larger institution. Barone, vice president of EDUCAUSE, writes about how new technologies affect teaching, learning, and the traditional institutional structures (Barone, 2003). She is far from alone in wrestling with the problem of how nontraditional programs like ELI should fit inside college structures that were developed when chalk was the dominant technology. Similarly, Muilenburg and Berge (2001) identify administrative structure and organizational change as primary barriers to distance learning. Levy's (2003) literature review also illustrates the complexity of issues involved in distance learning organizational structure and administrative procedures. Also, in a monograph commissioned by the American Council on Education (ACE) and EDUCAUSE, Oblinger, Barone, and Hawkins (2001) express concern about the "daunting" (p. 14) governance issues facing colleges and universities, and question whether existing models can react quickly enough, provide sufficient independence, and ensure integration.

Distance learning administrators are not the only ones concerned with organizational issues. In an article in *Business Officer,* Duin and others (2002) describe three basic organizational approaches to distance learning: adding bolt-on programs and new services to traditional units in order to support initiatives by innovative faculty (for example, adding support for Blackboard through the IT department), embedding programs in various units to transform the institution slowly and deliberately from within (such as adding instructional developers to traditional academic departments), and creating spin-off programs outside traditional institutional structures to establish a new culture with new incentives (for example, creating a separate distance learning unit).

ELI is an example of the spin-off approach. A number of authors have concluded that this tactic, although often unpopular among traditional units of the institution, may have significant advantages over other distance learning organizational structures (Duin and others, 2002; Heterick, Mingle, and Twigg, 1998; Hitt and Hartman, 2002; Oblinger, Barone, and Hawkins, 2001).

Ultimately, it is often the senior administrators who must structure distance learning to fit their own style and concepts of the way things should be run. As Hitt and Hartman (2002) put it, "Distributed learning initiatives require a change in leadership role and a different leadership style" (p. 9). Ward, president of ACE, and Hawkins, president of EDUCAUSE, sum it up well by pointing out that the practice of senior administrators staying out of technology discussions worked well during the "pioneering phase" (Ward and Hawkins, 2003, p. 39). However, now that technology is so central and strategic to the institution, presidents and other administrators must become engaged and involved in technology decision making.

ELI has not been immune to these challenges; its organizational placement inside the college has changed several times since it was created. Today, distance learning, technology training, application support, college technology planning, the college's technology help desk, as well as management of the college's Web site, maintenance of the college's technology infrastructure, and management of the college's servers are part of a unit that reports to a vice president of instructional and information technology. This organizational structure creates a synergy by keeping all technology support units together, although some faculty and academic administrators continue to feel strongly that the distance learning program should be housed directly under the academic administration. They want more control of the distance learning agenda and resources, but there is no agreement on exactly how that should be done. This tension often leads to internal debates far more complex than envisioned in ELI's earlier model.

Decision Making. ELI's original model recognized that just putting the right teams together would not be sufficient to support meaningful innovation; the actual decision-making process would also be important. The model recommended that projects be initiated by faculty with regular input from administration and faculty leaders to make sure the unit was in tune with the institution. It went on to recommend that the unit employ a flexible approach that is sensitive to faculty and institutional needs, that faculty participate in project decision making, and that written records of meetings, decisions, and agreements be kept (Sachs, 1984, p. 7).

ELI learned early on that allowing the college's full-time faculty to play a major role in distance learning course decision making was crucial to success. Most of these decisions centered on course design and use of instructional materials. Although both faculty and administrative input continue to be important today, the dynamic is different from when distance learning was still considered very innovative. In the early years, ELI was eager to support any interested faculty member, often playing the salesperson role with administrators to gain permission for a faculty member to develop and offer a distance learning course. Today, there are frequently more requests to support distance learning initiatives, venture into new technologies, or try bold new approaches than can readily be supported—at least all at once. This requires juggling resources to provide a consistent level of support while at the same time encouraging creativity and innovation. Beaudoin (2003) points out that the roles of "advocate, reformer, and technician" are becoming less critical in distance learning leadership, whereas the roles of "conceptualizer, implementer, and evaluator" remain as important as before (p. 12).

Another aspect of decision making not really envisioned in the original model is how well traditional college committee structures deal with technology and distance learning issues. Duderstadt, Atkins, and Van Houweling (2003) note that many of the faculty and administrators serving on these committees lack the technical knowledge and experience necessary to make truly informed decisions about distance learning. They further observe that many committee members are highly protective of the status quo or overly cautious at a time when technology is forcing responses at rates unprecedented in higher education. Yet "to be competitive and successful, distributed education will require a governance model with a level of dynamism and flexibility dramatically different from traditional faculty governance models" (Oblinger, Barone, and Hawkins, 2001, p. 13). Where once ELI could respond quickly to changes and opportunities, now it is often caught—sometimes by its own faculty—in a web that belies its innovative traditions. At ELI the solution, though imperfect, has been to actively form new alliances and partnerships in the college and to initiate more pilot projects than when it was newly established. These strategies tend to satisfy the various committees more than the strength of the projects themselves.

Involving faculty in decision making also raises other significant issues concerning intellectual property rights and ownership of distance learning courses. As opposed to questions of copyright or fair use in the production of materials—issues ELI dealt with during the early growth years—today's challenges center on who owns the distance learning courses developed and taught by individual faculty members but offered through ELI. Ownership was not originally a big problem for ELI because most faculty based their classes on telecourses licensed from commercial sources like the Adult Learning Service of the Public Broadcasting Service (PBS), televised lectures produced by the college's own television center, or commercially available textbooks and study guides. Now that many faculty produce online courses and course materials on their own PCs, ownership and property right issues have become less straightforward. The number of people writing about this subject is testament to its importance and complexity; the best advice has been to establish ownership up front (Gross, Gross, and Pirkl, 1998; Southern Regional Education Board, 2001; Levine and Sun, 2002; Levy, 2003).

For ELI, however, the issue is more complex than simply establishing ownership up front. For example, what constitutes a course in the online environment? Is a basic syllabus or a Blackboard site with posted assignments and discussion topics really of sufficient weight to be a course? At what point can a faculty member prevent another from using course material without permission? And when should input from an instructional developer be considered so significant that the faculty member is no longer the sole author of the material? There have been a number of cases when the advice of an instructional developer turned a faculty member's ideas into something truly valuable and worth owning, but it is difficult to quantify that advice and protect both faculty and college interests. In addition, there is the question of what constitutes fair compensation when ELI wants to use course materials that belong to a professor; the true market value is often far less than what the instructor assumes. To deal with these issues, ELI developed a policy describing the kinds of materials a faculty member can own (a simple syllabus or Blackboard site do not qualify), the conditions under which ELI will pay to use them, and the ways in which conflicts will be resolved (Extended Learning Institute, 2003).

A Work in Progress

When ELI was established, it focused on surviving and building enrollments; little thought was given to what would happen when success made it part of the mainstream. Even the model that outlined critical success factors for supporting innovation ignored the long-term issues, and with the passage of time and changes in staff, the original model was forgotten. The principles that led ELI to early success remain important, however, and many of them have made their way into formal and informal policies, procedures, and traditions. Nonetheless, new issues have emerged that require different strategies and different approaches. Unlike the original set of best practices, there is far less agreement on the best responses to these new challenges. Ironically, ELI again finds itself in uncharted waters—just as it did when it was a distance learning pioneer in the 1970s. So although ELI has made it to the mainstream, it remains a work in progress.

References

Barone, C. A. "The Changing Landscape and the New Academy." *EDUCAUSE Review,* Sep.-Oct. 2003, *38*(5), 40–47.

Beaudoin, M. F. "Distance Education Leadership for the New Century." *Online Journal of Distance Learning Administration,* Summer 2003, *VI*(II). http://www.westga.edu/%7Edistance/ojdla/summer62/beaudoin62.html. Accessed Aug. 12, 2004.

Compora, D. P. "Current Trends in Distance Education: An Administrative Model." *Online Journal of Distance Learning Administration,* Summer 2003, *VI*(II). http://www.westga.edu/%7Edistance/ojdla/summer62/compora62.html. Accessed Aug. 12, 2004.

Duderstadt, J. J., Atkins, D. E., and Van Houweling, D. "The Development of Institutional Strategies." *EDUCAUSE Review,* May-June 2003, *38*(3), 48–58.

Duin, A. H., and others. "Moving Forward with Distance Education." *Business Officer,* May 2002, *35*(11), 19–23.

Extended Learning Institute. *ELI Guide for Faculty: Teaching a Course.* Annandale: Northern Virginia Community College, June 2003. http://eli.nvcc.edu/pdf/ELIGuideTeachingFaculty6–03.pdf. Accessed Aug. 12, 2004.

Gross, R., Gross, D., and Pirkl, R. *New Connections: A Guide to Distance Education.* Washington, D.C.: Instructional Telecommunications Council, 1998.

Heterick, R. C., Mingle, J. R., and Twigg, C. A. "The Public Policy Implications of a Global Learning Infrastructure." Report from a Joint NLII-SHEEO Symposium, Denver, Colo., Nov. 1997. Washington, D.C.: Educom, 1998. http://www.educause.edu/ir/library/html/nli0005.html. Accessed Aug. 12, 2004.

Hitt, J. C., and Hartman, J. L. *Distributed Learning: New Challenges and Opportunities for Institutional Leadership.* Washington, D.C.: American Council on Education, 2002.

Levine, A., and Sun, J. C. *Barriers to Distance Education.* Washington, D.C.: American Council on Education, 2002.

Levine, T. K., Gallagher, P. J., Boccuti, C., and Meyer, T. T. *Going the Distance: A Handbook for Developing Distance Degree Programs Using Television Courses and Telecommunications Technologies.* Washington, D.C.: Annenberg CPB Project, 1992.

Levy, S. "Six Factors to Consider When Planning Online Distance Learning Programs in Higher Education." *Online Journal of Distance Learning Administration,* Spring 2003, VI(I). http://www.westga.edu/%7Edistance/ojdla/spring61/levy61.htm. Accessed Aug. 12, 2004.

Muilenburg, L., and Berge, Z. L. "Barriers to Distance Education: A Factor-Analytic Study." *American Journal of Distance Education,* 2001, 15(2), 7–22.

O'Banion, T. "Sustaining Innovation in Teaching and Learning." *Leadership Abstracts,* 7(4). http://www.league.org/publication/abstracts/leadership/labs0494.htm. Accessed Aug. 12, 2004.

Oblinger, D. G., Barone, C. A., and Hawkins, B. L. *Distributed Education and Its Challenges: An Overview.* Washington, D.C.: American Council on Education, 2001.

Sachs, S. G. *Supporting Real Innovation in the '80s—Characteristics of ID Units That Will Make It Happen.* Washington, D.C.: Association for Educational Communications and Technology, Division for Instructional Development, 1984. (ED 267 729)

Sachs, S. G. "The Mature Distance Education Program: Which Way Now?" *Performance Improvement Quarterly,* 1999, 12(2), 66–83.

Southern Regional Education Board, Distance Learning Policy Laboratory, Faculty Issues Subcommittee. *Supporting Faculty in the Use of Technology: A Guide to Principles, Policies, and Implementation Strategies.* Atlanta: Southern Regional Education Board, 2001. http://www.electroniccampus.org/policylab/Reports/Supporting_Faculty.pdf. Accessed Aug. 12, 2004.

Ward, D., and Hawkins, B. L. "Presidential Leadership for Information Technology." *EDUCAUSE Review,* May-June 2003, 38(3), 36–39.

STEVEN G. SACHS *is vice president of instructional and information technology at Northern Virginia Community College.*

4

Community colleges are well positioned to provide underserved student populations with access to computer technology. This chapter explores the issues of access and technology from multiple perspectives in the community college, and explains how community colleges can develop a foundation for their technology plan.

Access and Technology

Lemuel W. Watson

America has never provided equal access to technology for all individuals. Limited resources and market-driven demand consistently help create gaps in access to new goods. As Light (2001) asserts, "From electricity to the telephone and the automobile, most technologies did not enter U.S. society equitably" (p. 711). Higher education has been no exception. Once considered a luxury, access to higher education has become widely available with the proliferation of open admissions community colleges. However, a new and different gap has developed—a "digital divide," or disparity in access to technology.

In a society increasingly shaped by technology, students who are constrained by time and place, or are otherwise disadvantaged, are being left behind (Matthews, 1999). According to Moore (2002), "Access [to higher education] was originally thought of as the ability to gain entrance to an institution or program. The concept gradually shifted from one of equity in admissions to equity in outcomes, or the ability of a student or group of students to succeed once admitted" (p. 1). Thus, gaining entrance to a college or program, although necessary, is no longer sufficient, because in addition to traditional academic skills, students now need technology skills to compete in a changing job market.

This chapter examines the role of the community college in bridging the digital divide and providing access to technology for disadvantaged populations. Although bridging the digital divide promises many benefits for individuals, institutions, and communities, evidence of success should be examined carefully, because "technology is not a neutral tool with universal effects, but rather a medium with consequences that are significantly shaped by the historical, social, and cultural context of its use" (Light, 2001, p. 711).

The Digital Divide Personified

New users of technology usually exhibit four stages of readiness to access and use educational technology. The first stage is recognizing that technology could enhance the efficiency, productivity, or quality of their personal and professional lives. The second stage is becoming open to learning about information technology and learning to apply hardware and software to the task at hand. In the third stage, users seek physical access to an appropriate technological infrastructure. In stage four, users actively follow through on the decision to use technology.

There are many disparities between students at the first stage of readiness and those at the fourth. A student at the fourth stage may feel comfortable using a computer for an assignment or taking a distance learning course, but a student at the first stage may not feel comfortable with or able to take advantage of either opportunity. Take the example of a student living in a rural area of a southern state. This single mother of two, who works full time in a textile mill, decides to go back to school at the local community college. She has not had any exposure (access) to technology other than cable television. Her first college assignment is to write a one-page biographical sketch and to send it to the instructor as an e-mail attachment. The student writes her biographical sketch longhand and gives it to the instructor at the next class. He gives her a C. He also indicates on the paper that she is to repeat the assignment, type it, and send it to him via e-mail before the next class. She feels lost. Why? Because she has never used a computer. Compounding that feeling, she does not even know where to get an e-mail account or how to use an e-mail software program. Computers were not a part of her last academic experience some twenty years earlier.

This student is at the first stage of technology readiness and access, and personifies the far edge of the digital divide. She must be encouraged and supported in building her ability to use technology to complete her courses and degree. Although she is provided with access to technology through her college's computer labs, she did not even think to utilize this resource. This student will have to invest an enormous amount of effort and time to become efficient and productive in the basic technology skills needed for success in her coursework. How quickly she will acclimate to technology and become productive depends on her initial experiences, motivation, and support. Will she find the funds to purchase a computer for her home? Or will she have to find time to use the computer lab between work and caring for her children? Will she have the time to take a basic computer course in order to learn how to efficiently use technology, even though it will not count toward her degree?

The community college is one of the few institutions that gives disadvantaged students a chance to obtain a college education and provides adult learners with affordable opportunities to continue lifelong learning. Providing access to technology is complex because people have varying needs and levels of exposure to technology. However, one consequence of the digital divide is that many people are not fully aware of the benefits of technology and how it might enhance their personal and working lives. Educating these learners, and providing them with access to and support for technology, is the first step in bridging the digital divide.

The Relationship Between Demographics and Access

Patterns of Internet usage reveal significant disparities in access to technology along demographic lines. For example, a Pew Foundation survey (Madden, 2003) indicated that half of all adults eighteen years and older in the United States (ninety-four million) do not have Internet access at home. These individuals are more likely to be nonwhite and less likely to be financially well-off. Only 31 percent of Americans whose households earn less than $30,000 per year have access to the Internet at home. Conversely, more than three-quarters (78 percent) of those living in households earning more than $75,000 per year have Internet access (Madden, 2003).

In addition, whites are more likely than any other racial or ethnic group to have Internet access at home. Roughly 50 percent of whites have access to the Internet, compared with 36 percent of blacks and 44 percent of Hispanics. In most respects, however, ethnic and racial variances can be explained by differences in income. Wealthier whites, blacks, and Hispanics are online at roughly the same rates in households earning more than $75,000 (78 percent of whites, 79 percent of Hispanics, and 69 percent of blacks). Similarly, 32 percent of whites in households earning less than $30,000 are online, compared with 25 percent of blacks and 26 percent of Hispanics (Madden, 2003).

Access to technology also varies by level of educational attainment: more than two-thirds (71 percent) of those who do not have Internet access at home have only a high school diploma or less. In contrast, only one-third (32 percent) of Internet users have only a high school diploma or less. Thus, individuals without Internet access usually report having lower levels of educational attainment than Internet users.

Where one lives in the country also appears to influence one's place in the digital divide. Regions with the highest rates of Internet penetration are the Pacific Northwest (68 percent of residents have access to the Internet), New England (66 percent), and California (65 percent). Internet usage lags somewhat in the southeastern states (57 percent), and in the industrial Midwest (55 percent). The South (48 percent) demonstrates the lowest levels of Internet usage (Madden, 2003). According to Tapscott (1998), a great deal of this disparity can be attributed to socioeconomic status. Despite the various reasons for disparities in access, however, community colleges must work to build an infrastructure that supports access to technology for all students.

Building an Infrastructure to Provide Access

Presently, community colleges are facing critical decisions about how information technology fits within their organizations. Administrators and technology leaders must ask: How will or should technology be used in our college? Who will need access and for what? What are our short- and long-term goals? Colleges that are successful in answering these questions are better able to integrate technology into their instructional and administrative life. Effective leadership and solid strategic planning help ensure success in this effort (Rush, 1996; Ryland, 2000; Wenger, 1996). Good planning includes conducting research, examining external resources, facilitating internal discussion, detailing specifics, and setting timetables and deadlines.

Create an Information Technology Plan. An information technology (IT) plan should be driven by the college's mission and should build on institutional commitments to other financial, educational, and human resource plans. IT plans should be descriptive, detailed, and institution-specific, and they should address issues of organizational change, technology upgrades, cost, and the involvement of constituents, experts, and necessary human resources. IT plans should also discuss how technology will be integrated into the college's overall infrastructure (Wenger, 1996).

Electronic Data Systems, an information technology services provider, has developed what it calls a System Life Cycle (SLC), which helps organizations integrate technology into their infrastructure. The SLC uses the following questions to develop an IT plan for clients: What are the processes the institution engages in each day? Should the processes be automated or not? What are the benefits of automating? Are the investments worth the cost? What are the basic hardware, software, and training needs to operate the system efficiently? Have we asked the right people and the right questions so that the organization fully understands how to develop a system that will address its needs? Although these questions are simple, they ensure that an institution understands the complex and intertwined maze of people and processes involved. In addition, community colleges need to ask for the perspective of students, faculty, and staff in order to implement a successful technology access plan.

Provide Access. In addition to developing a strong technology plan, community colleges must provide what Wenger (1996) identifies as the four main levels of access to technology. First, the college must develop and provide technological resources and support services for students. These may include dial-up services or a help desk. A resource center that offers basic skills courses and training is often very helpful for students who are not familiar with technology.

Second, faculty need to be provided with access to technology so they can create curriculum and course materials for both on- and off-campus courses. In addition, faculty must be given access to institutional hardware and software if they are to help students negotiate the system. Faculty should have a voice in the development and maintenance of any technology system to ensure that it meets their needs.

Third, administrators should be provided with broad levels of access so that they can obtain information from all systems in the institution and use that data in their reporting and decision making. Fourth, a central computer network technology process should be designed and implemented in order to manage administrative and instructional processes for staff, faculty, and students. In addition to these four levels of access, community colleges should allow for feedback whenever possible. Student and faculty feedback on access issues should be directed to the administrator in charge of maintaining and improving technology systems.

Best Practices

Many community colleges have profited from good planning and leadership in developing access to technology. The Community College of Denver has developed a state-of-the-art internal network system that has considerably increased access. Similarly, Macomb Community College (Georgia) has put its entire enrollment process online. Waubonsee Community College (Illinois) offers private tutors for students, faculty, or staff who are not as technologically literate as they would like to be, and the North Carolina Community College System has introduced a very detailed, deadline-oriented technology plan that contains fifteen goals and objectives. As well, Miami-Dade College is making changes that will allow more synchronicity between the college and the state reporting system, enabling better communication between state and educational leaders.

Illinois has also taken steps to build an infrastructure for technology access, and has planned to have its forty-eight community colleges share courses and resources (Carnevale, 2000). The state has established the Illinois Community Colleges Online (ILCCO) initiative, a statewide online degree or certificate program. Its mission is to expand access to learning opportunities for all residents of Illinois, independent of location or time. ILCCO provides a wide range of online learning opportunities to Illinois residents at a reasonable cost and allows students at any community college to access, through their home campus, online courses and programs delivered by other community colleges in the state (http://www.iccb.state.il.us/ilcco/faq.html). Common to ILCCO and the other colleges mentioned here are a strong technology plan and experts who can assist in developing a system that is adaptable and flexible enough to deal with a dynamic technological environment.

Concluding Thoughts and Suggestions

Because of the variety of funding configurations for community colleges, it is difficult to provide universally applicable recommendations to improve access to technology. However, the following suggestions, derived from my experiences with technology as well as my understanding of the literature on technology in community colleges, may be helpful to those colleges concerned about providing access to technology for all students.

Work to Narrow the Digital Divide. Community colleges should "monitor progress toward equal access" (Gladieux and Swail, 2002, p. 535). Maintaining access will continue to be a key issue for two-year colleges. They are the nation's gateway to higher education and must remain committed to the open door policy, even as educational standards change and associated requirements increase. Although improving access sometimes conflicts with increasing institutional productivity (Gilbert, 1996), community colleges should commit themselves to a basic standard for access to technology.

Make Access the Core of Systems Design. Community colleges should "consider broad access in the development of products and the expansion of markets" (Gladieux and Swail, 2002, p. 535). Access for those who use, maintain, and develop technology should be one of the most important components of a community college system. Therefore, colleges should frequently evaluate and enhance access for students, faculty, administrators, and staff. Because information doubles every seven years, workers must be constantly retrained, companies must be reengineered, and colleges must help prepare a workforce that is technologically competent. Colleges must also be flexible, enlist community partners, and emphasize learning outcomes instead of teaching inputs (Oblinger, 1996). Community colleges must attempt to understand and resolve the complex problems and potentials associated with providing access in an era of technological change.

Develop Leaders Who Understand How to Manage Information Technology. Community colleges must develop leaders who understand how to use technology to enhance student learning, enhance the productivity of faculty and staff, and increase the efficiency of the college in general. This type of leadership is needed if colleges are to reap the benefits of technology (Rush, 1996). The initial step in this process is philosophical, and should include reflection on beliefs about learning (Desjardins, 2001) as well as acknowledgment of the potential impact of technology.

Keep the Promise of Technology in Perspective. Community colleges should "learn from the distance-learning pioneers" (Gladieux and Swail, 2002, p. 535) and plan carefully for cost, access, and usage. They must be patient and allow the pioneer institutions to be the first to test new technologies. They must be sure to discover and resolve any problems before taking on the expense of purchasing new software or hardware.

Evaluate Accountability to the Community. Community colleges are renowned for their ability to adapt quickly to changing technology and community needs. However, with increasing calls for educational accountability, it is necessary for institutional leaders to ask themselves difficult questions as they plan, maintain, and enhance access to technology for students and the community. For example, what role will the college play in providing access to technology in a community? If ensuring community access to technology is one of its roles, who should bear the costs? What are the educational gains or outcomes? Finally, what minimum level of access to technology should the college provide? To stay true to their missions, when community colleges work to provide access to technology they must make every effort to ensure that quality and cost work together to enhance educational outcomes (Fleit, 1994). In other words, technology is not an end in and of itself. Rather it is a means by which community colleges can better fulfill their responsibility to provide access to all students and to the community at large.

References

Carnevale, D. "Community Colleges in Illinois Seek to Share Their Courses Online." *Chronicle of Higher Education,* Mar. 24, 2000, 46(29), A52. http://chronicle.com/prm/weekly/v46/i29/29a05201.htm. Accessed Aug. 13, 2004.

Desjardins, C. *The Leading Edge: Competencies for Community College Leadership in the New Millennium.* Mission Viejo, Calif.: League for Innovation in the Community College, 2001.

Fleit, L. H. *Self-Assessment for Campus Information Technology Services.* CAUSE Professional Paper Series, No. 12. Boulder, Colo.: CAUSE, 1994.

Gilbert, S. "Double Visions: Paradigms in Balance or Collision?" *Change,* 1996, 28(2), 8–11.

Gladieux, L. E., and Swail, W. S. "The Virtual University and Educational Opportunity: Issues of Equity and Access for the Next Generation." In L. Foster, B. L. Bower, and L. W. Watson (eds.), *ASHE Reader—Distance Education: Teaching and Learning in Higher Education* (pp. 526–543). Boston: Pearson Custom, 2002.

Light, J. S. "Rethinking the Digital Divide." *Harvard Educational Review,* 2001, 71(4), 709–733.

Madden, M. "America's Online Pursuits: The Changing Picture of Who's Online and What They Do." In L. Rainie (ed.), *Pew Internet and American Life Project.* Philadelphia, Pa.: Pew Charitable Trusts, 2003. http://www.pewtrusts.com/pdf/pew_internet_yearend_2003.pdf. Accessed Aug. 16, 2004.

Matthews, D. "The Origins of Distance Education and Its Use in the United States." *Technological Horizons in Education Journal,* 1999, 27(2), 54–67.

Moore, P. L. *Access and Success in Web Courses at an Urban Multicultural Community College: The Student's Perspective.* Unpublished research report, Northern Arizona University, 2002. (ED 465 402)

Oblinger, D. G. "Creating a Learning Culture." In L. Johnson and S. T. Lobello (eds.), *The 21st Century Community College: Technology and the New Learning Paradigm.* Mission Viejo, Calif.: League for Innovation in the Community College, 1996.

Rush, S. C. "The Importance of Process Innovation to the Community College." In L. Johnson and S. T. Lobello (eds.), *The 21st Century Community College: Technology and the New Learning Paradigm.* Mission Viejo, Calif.: League for Innovation in the Community College, 1996.

Ryland, J. N. *Technology and the Future of the Community College. New Expeditions: Charging the Second Century of Community Colleges.* Issues Paper No. 10. Washington, D.C.: American Association of Community Colleges, 2000. (ED 439 744)

Tapscott, D. *Growing Up Digital: The Rise of the Net Generation.* New York: McGraw-Hill, 1998.

Wenger, G. E. "Planning to Take Advantage of Technology." In L. Johnson and S. T. Lobello (eds.), *The 21st Century Community College: Technology and the New Learning Paradigm*. Mission Viejo, Calif.: League for Innovation in the Community College, 1996.

LEMUEL W. WATSON *is professor of higher education and chair of the department of counseling, adult, and higher education at Northern Illinois University in DeKalb. He recently spent time as a Fulbright Scholar at the National Institute of Higher Education at Belarusian State University.*

5

This chapter describes strategies for containing and reducing the costs of e-learning through cost identification, appropriate instructional roles, course development, program scale, and course redesign.

Five Important Lessons About the Cost of E-Learning

Carol Scarafiotti

Rio Salado College (Arizona), one of the ten Maricopa community colleges, is recognized nationally for its successful distance learning program, which consists primarily of electronically delivered learning (e-learning). This program, which began in 1996 with six thousand students, currently serves twenty-one thousand individuals per year. Rio Salado's e-learning program provides students with high-quality online courses, programs, and services that are conveniently available at an affordable price. The tuition for e-learning courses is the same as for face-to-face courses: $55 per credit hour for in-state students and $135 per credit hour for out-of-state learners. With just under half its total enrollment offered through e-learning, Rio Salado College operates at a cost that is 34 percent below the average of its nine sister colleges. It is able to do so because it has developed and implemented several e-learning cost-containment strategies. This chapter describes five important lessons that Rio Salado College, a participant in the Pew-sponsored Center for Academic Transformation's course redesign project, learned about the cost of e-learning and strategies for containing these costs.

Lesson One: Identify E-Learning Costs

Unlike in a traditional face-to-face class where an instructor is responsible for all tasks related to developing and delivering a course, e-learning involves a variety of resources, all of which have associated costs. Colleges looking for rules of thumb on e-learning costs, or for comparative data from other colleges, should proceed with caution and be aware that e-learning costs will vary according to institutional goals and approaches. Nonetheless, a formal costing methodology can provide guidance in identifying the costs of e-learning.

The Technology Costing Methodology is one such method. Developed by Dennis Jones through the National Center for Higher Education Management Systems and the Western Cooperative for Educational Telecommunications, it is free to users and available online (http://www.wcet. info/projects/tcm). This methodology was designed to apply to a variety of technology-assisted delivery modes, and helps colleges to identify the activities directly associated with their unique e-learning approaches, as well as the full range of costs associated with those activities.

Another costing methodology, assisted cost calculation (Jones, 2001), focuses on broad areas of organizational structure—instruction, academic support, student services, and institutional support—that are then divided into subcategories. For example, instruction is divided into course design and development, instructional materials, content delivery, tutoring, and assessment.

Jones's methodology includes factors that affect the bottom line, such as costs borne by others, the costs of unused capacity, and the costs of adding capacity (Jones, 2001). This methodology also gives institutions the choice of analyzing costs by course, discipline, or type of delivery. This unit of analysis feature is important because it helps colleges match the cost analysis to their particular e-learning circumstances. For example, colleges with very large e-learning systems containing multiple programs, large numbers of courses, and high enrollments may opt to analyze cost by delivery mode. Colleges offering only limited numbers of programs or courses via e-learning, however, may choose to analyze costs by course. Whatever unit of analysis is selected, the final calculation results in cost per student per credit hour for that unit.

Rio Salado College uses a costing model similar to the Technology Costing Methodology but one that recognizes that e-learning is one of the college's primary missions. Just under half of Rio Salado's total credit enrollments come from the e-learning program's 230 individual courses. These courses feed into twenty-one certificate and twelve degree programs, as well as two postbaccalaureate pathways. To support e-learning, the college provides all requisite student services; enrollment assistance, advising, counseling, and the bookstore are available online and via the phone six days a week while the instructional and technology support help desks, tutoring, and the library are available seven days a week. As well, the college provides a range of services for e-learning faculty, such as course development and production advice and training for adjunct faculty.

Given the large scope of its e-learning program, Rio Salado's costing methodology relates costs to the entire e-learning program instead of to individual courses. Also, because the college's e-learning enrollments are so large, it is not affected by the cost of unused capacity. Rio Salado calculates direct and indirect costs per full-time enrollment equivalent (FTEE; the total annual credit hours divided by thirty), which is a common measure used in Maricopa's budgeting process. In this methodology, the direct costs of e-learning-associated services, such as course development, are apportioned by the FTEE.

Lesson Two: Explore Ways to Maximize Human Resources

Sally Johnstone and Russell Poulin, who have studied institutions using the Technology Costing Methodology, note that "the most critical variables affecting the cost of using technology in teaching and learning activities all relate to people"—what they do and what they are paid (2002, p. 14). Rio Salado College, designed at its inception to deliver instruction primarily with adjunct faculty, exemplifies Johnstone and Poulin's finding on human resource costs. Today the college's e-learning instructional staff includes over four hundred adjunct faculty members and twenty-seven full-time faculty chairs.

How does this affect the bottom line? Higher-paid, full-time faculty chairs with tremendous experience in e-learning pedagogy and instructional design develop Rio Salado's online courses, while adjunct faculty members do most of the teaching. Full-time faculty chairs orient adjunct faculty to the already developed courses, and also train, mentor, and evaluate the adjunct faculty. They establish e-learning policies such as expectations for faculty communication responsiveness. The guidance and support of faculty chairs, as well as the use of previously developed courses, ensure that adjunct faculty members provide high-quality instruction. Because the cost of a three-credit course taught by an adjunct faculty member is 69 percent less than if it is taught by a full-time professor, Rio Salado is able to provide quality instruction while minimizing human resource costs.

In addition, the college has structured its resources to ensure that the adjunct faculty members' time is spent on teaching and learning activities, rather than on nonteaching tasks such as developing courses, answering technology questions, or orienting students to the college's e-learning system. For example, the college has provided two help desks that students can contact for assistance. Students with technology problems are encouraged to call or e-mail the technology help desk rather than the instructor, and students who have questions about course logistics, such as flexibility with assignment dates or test times, are encouraged to call the instructional support help desk to get assistance from adjunct faculty who are trained to answer such questions. Also, Rio Salado's faculty chairs serve as mentors to all online adjunct faculty, which ensures that the adjuncts know how to take advantage of the college's many support services. With this type of support for Rio Salado's adjunct faculty, the college can in good conscience require enrollment loads of twenty-five to thirty-five students per faculty member, depending on the complexity of the course. This level of enrollment in e-learning courses also helps contain costs.

Lesson Three: Implement Policies to Help Contain Course Development and Production Costs

According to a national survey on distance education at degree-granting postsecondary institutions, the cost of course development is the number one factor that prevents an institution from starting or expanding distance education course offerings (U.S. Department of Education, 2003). Unlike a face-to-face course, which the instructor designs alone, developing an e-learning course can mean involving programmers, Web technicians, graphic artists, instructional designers, content specialists, editors, course testers, copyright usage checkers, and others. It is no wonder that Johnstone and Poulin (2002) warn, "If we are going to have really good electronically mediated courses, then we need to accept the high costs of designing and developing them" (p. 18). With this in mind, colleges need some strategies to contain or justify the costs of developing electronic courses.

In order to maximize Rio Salado College's investment in courses delivered over the Web, the college's policy is to develop one master course that is taught by numerous faculty members over a three-year period. This approach to course development has both fiscal and instructional advantages. From a fiscal perspective, the college can amortize the course development and production costs over thousands of students who enroll during the lifetime of the course. From an instructional perspective, the college can afford to invest significantly in the development of one excellent master course. If, in contrast, a college supports the development of numerous versions of the same course, the cost will escalate and the college's ability to invest in course development will diminish. For example, in order to serve 3,600 students over a three-year period, a college might spend $2,000 in development costs for each of seventeen versions of Psychology 101 (225 students per version). Although it spends a total of $34,000, it is investing only $2,000 in each course. In contrast, the same 3,600 students could be served over a three-year period with one version of Psychology 101. In this case, because the college develops only one course, it can use up to $34,000 to create a high-quality course that can be delivered as many times as needed over the three years.

Lesson Four: Consider Scale and Scalability

The scale of an e-learning program is measured by the sheer number of students enrolled in it. Scalability, in contrast, refers to an organization's capacity to adequately serve large and increasing numbers of e-learning students. Large-scale enrollments drive down fixed costs. Kevin Kruse (2002–2004) correctly portrays scale as a significant element in determining initial course development costs and makes the point that "the cost is the same regardless of whether there will be ten students or a thousand" (p. 8). Enrollment scalability is also an important consideration in the development of support services for e-learning. That is, colleges that have or are anticipating large enrollments can justify implementing a full range of services, whereas colleges with small enrollments may need to find more cost-effective methods.

Rio Salado College's e-learning program was designed for large-scale enrollments and a scalable support system. In 1995, Rio Salado chose to make distance learning a primary focus of its mission. Among the first actions associated with this change were the dismantling of its small ancillary distance learning department—which functioned in isolation—and the creation of a collegewide system to support distance learning, primarily e-learning. Today, visitors to Rio Salado College are often surprised to find there is no distance learning department. Instead, they find course development, production and support, information services, faculty hiring services, an instructional support help desk that includes online tutoring, a technology support help desk, and student enrollment services, all supporting Rio's e-learning faculty and students online or over the phone. Because the e-learning program was designed in anticipation of growth, Rio Salado College has a system of services scaled to meet the needs of its growing body of students. Colleges with small numbers of e-learning enrollments can avoid the costs of expensive infrastructure and services by participating in e-learning consortia that provide such services or by outsourcing course development or other services such as a technology help desk.

Lesson Five: Redesign Large-Enrollment Courses to Reduce Cost and Improve Learning

In 1999, Rio Salado College was selected to participate in the Center for Academic Transformation's course redesign project, funded by the Pew Charitable Trusts ("Pew Learning and Technology Program," 2002). This program, spearheaded by Carol Twigg, funded a variety of colleges and universities to prove that the use of technology in higher education could not only increase access and reduce costs but also improve learning. Over a three-year period, thirty institutions explored ways to redesign large-enrollment courses to accomplish these goals. In addition to redesigning a large course, each participating college had to compare its costs and learning outcomes to the same course provided in a traditional format. Of the thirty course redesign projects, five—including Rio Salado's—were fully online.

The Pew redesign project required that each institution focus on improving student learning, make detailed financial plans, and meet basic readiness criteria (Twigg, 1999). Each college had to demonstrate it was ready to participate in course redesign from both institutional and instructional perspectives. Institutional readiness criteria required proof of the organization's desire to reduce or control costs, an adequate information technology infrastructure, and a commitment to learner-centered education. Likewise, the instructional readiness criteria necessitated providing evidence of a substantial number of faculty members with experience in computer-based instruction, a willingness to experiment, courses with the potential for "capital-for-labor substitution," and a plan to "support the ongoing operation of the redesigned course" (Twigg, 1999, pp. 9–10).

Having met most of the instructional readiness criteria, Rio Salado College decided to redesign its Internet-delivered introductory algebra course, a prerequisite for students needing to complete college algebra, and third on the Maricopa list of the top twenty-five largest enrollment courses. At the time, Rio Salado College was using Academic Systems, a CD-ROM technology, to deliver its pre-algebra and college algebra courses over the Internet. This software presented interactive course content including customized homework assignments related to individual student performance. It also provided the faculty member with information about each student's progress, and tracked each student's time on task. Prior to the course redesign project, Rio Salado's online math courses using Academic Systems software were staffed and supported in the same way as other online courses; one instructor was responsible for thirty-five students.

In exploring ways in which introductory algebra could be redesigned, Rio Salado's math faculty chair and several adjunct faculty members—all experts in the use of Academic Systems—made several observations that influenced the planning of a new course delivery model. First, they agreed that they were not making full use of Academic Systems' student progress data. They felt that if they used the tracking data to communicate more often with students at critical junctures in the course, they could increase the course completion rate (which was then at 59 percent). Second, they noted that the instructional design and content of the Academic Systems math software worked well for most students, and that students relied on the instructors mainly to answer questions about course logistics, such as when to take tests. Thus, they decided it was possible to increase the number of students in the online Academic Systems class, and they committed to a redesign goal of increasing the number of students in a course from thirty-five to one hundred, while also increasing the course completion rate.

However, Rio Salado's twenty-six enrollment periods caused enrollments to be spread out over a semester, which made it impossible to provide one instructor with one hundred students at one time. Yet because Academic Systems also provided the content for three other courses—mathematical concepts and applications, intermediate algebra, and college algebra functions—these courses were added to the project. As a result, Rio Salado piloted a model in which one instructor used Academic Systems software to instruct one hundred students enrolled in any of these four math courses. A course assistant, a junior-level math major, was added to the course redesign in order to increase proactive communication with students. Using Academic Systems' built-in course management system, the course assistant monitored student progress and alerted the instructor to student difficulties with the material, thus helping the instructor take timely action with students who were lagging behind.

By using technology to its full capacity, increasing class size, offloading course management tasks to a course assistant, and devoting faculty time to four different but concurrent courses, Rio Salado realized a cost-per-student reduction of 37 percent (from $49 to $31 per student) compared with previous distance learning formats at the college. Overall, the course completion rate for the students in the redesigned course was 64.8 percent—a 5.8 percent increase from the previous standard. Rio Salado's success in increasing completion rates while tripling the number of students illustrates the potential of course redesign.

The redesigned course format of one hundred students per instructional assistance team was piloted with three different adjunct faculty members. Although it worked, and all three instructors had similar student completion rates, one faculty member did not feel comfortable working with the assistant and instead tended to answer questions and deal with issues that could have been delegated. As a result, this instructor became overwhelmed by one hundred students. Recognizing that there is variability among adjunct faculty members' ability to use the course management system and to adapt to one hundred students and an assistant, the college has since reduced the enrollment per faculty member to fifty, still saving nearly 19 percent over traditional e-learning courses.

Rio Salado College gained much from its Pew redesign experience. Interestingly, in retrospect the college's most valuable lesson was its realization that it too was vulnerable to the more costly approach of adding technology without changing the design of the course. Without the impetus of the Pew experience, the college might still be using Academic Systems software in a traditional course format with only thirty-five students per instructor.

Conclusion

Colleges seeking to contain or reduce the costs of e-learning programs will benefit from taking the time to carefully plan a strategy that is in alignment with their goals and program scope. That strategy begins with determining readiness for such an endeavor, and then using a technology costing methodology to determine its true costs. It goes on to explore cost-effective instructional roles and ways to contain the cost of online course development. A cost-containment strategy requires institutions to come to terms with the realities of scale. It may also necessitate redesigning the traditional course format in order to take full advantage of cost savings associated with technology. Ideally, institutions will develop a strategy that reduces cost while also improving learning.

References

Johnstone, S. M., and Poulin, R. "What Does Distance Learning Really Cost?" *Community College Journal*, 2002, 73(2) 14–20.

Jones, D. *Technology Costing Methodology Handbook.* Boulder, Colo.: Western Cooperative for Educational Telecommunications, 2001. http://www.wcet.info/projects/tcm. Accessed Aug. 13, 2004.

Kruse, K. "Beginner Basics: Measuring the Total Cost of E-Learning" *e-Learning Guru Newsletter,* 2002–2004. http://www.e-Learningguru.com/articles/art5_2.htm. Accessed May 7, 2004.

"Pew Learning and Technology Program: Center for Academic Transformation," 2002. http://www.center.rpi.edu/PewHome.html. Accessed Aug. 13, 2004.

Twigg, C. *Improving Learning & Reducing Costs: Redesigning Large-Enrollment Courses.* Troy, N.Y.: Center for Academic Transformation, Rensselaer Polytechnic Institute, 1999.

U.S. Department of Education, National Center for Education Statistics. *Distance Education at Degree-Granting Postsecondary Institutions: 2000–2001.* Washington, D.C.: U.S. Department of Education, 2003. http://nces.ed.gov/surveys/peqis/publications/2003017/. Accessed Aug. 13, 2004.

CAROL SCARAFIOTTI *is dean of instruction at Rio Salado College, a Maricopa Community College in Tempe, Arizona.*

6

As community college faculty become more involved with online courses, questions are emerging about pedagogy, workload, intellectual property, and a number of other issues. This chapter examines how the online environment has affected faculty work life.

Instructional and Work Life Issues for Distance Learning Faculty

Kimberly P. Hardy, Beverly L. Bower

Although education over the Internet has existed since the mid-1980s, only recently has e-learning become an integral part of higher education instruction (Simonson, Smaldino, Albright, and Zvacek, 2000). The Internet provides a way for students to communicate electronically with the instructor and other students in the class, and acts as a pathway to endless resources and information. It also provides convenient access to students who normally would not be able to obtain an education because of geographical distance or personal circumstances.

Teaching online requires a different pedagogy from that of the traditional classroom, as well as a unique set of skills (Fetherston, 2001; LaMonica, 2001; Oliver, 2002). Producing quality courses through this medium involves a great deal more than using a computer and posting class notes to a Web site. Instructors teaching over the Internet need to fit their methods to the requirements of the online environment, because students learn not only from the instructor in this setting but also through interactions with other students and resources (Arreola, 1995; Menges, 1994; Oliver, 2002).

The increasing popularity of online courses in community colleges has forced faculty and administrators alike to acknowledge and contend with a variety of issues. This chapter looks at changes in the instructor's role, workload and professional development issues, course organization and format, interacting and communicating with students, teaching and assessment methods, and intellectual property issues. It is necessary to address all of these issues in order to facilitate the learning process through this medium and improve teaching effectiveness.

The Teaching Role

Perhaps one of the biggest changes for community college faculty when they adapt a course to the online environment is the significant shift in their role (Dillon and Walsh, 1992). When they use the technology in a productive and effective manner, online faculty tend to take a greater role in assisting rather than informing their students. As Zukas (1999) found, students in online courses are more interested in discussing topics with other students than with their instructor—a somewhat different dynamic than that which exists in a traditional classroom. Because of this, and because content is easily accessible on course Web sites, the online instructor serves as a mentor, coordinator, and facilitator of learning rather than a conveyor of information. As O'Banion (1997) noted, the role of the learning facilitator must be defined by the needs of the learners. Thus, online instructors must provide experiences that increase learners' higher-order cognitive skills as opposed to simply transferring content to them (Gillespie, 1998).

According to a report from the American Association of Community Colleges (2000), to accommodate this new method of teaching, faculty must concentrate on creating the appropriate climate and learning conditions for their students, in addition to setting goals and sequencing content. They need to find a balance between the traditional role of information provider and the new role of facilitator, who guides discussion and provides online interactive learning experiences.

This shift in roles is a challenge for some faculty, and institutions that are increasing the number of Web-based courses offered have a responsibility to provide faculty with resources and training to assist in this role evolution. Furthermore, professional development programs must go beyond helping faculty convert materials and develop learning strategies for students and must directly address the more interactive role of the online instructor.

Workload and Faculty Development

Besides the change in role, faculty who teach online also experience a change in workload. Community college faculty have long realized that teaching in a Web-based environment requires a significant amount of time, generally more than that needed for a traditional course. First, faculty must put in the extra time necessary to develop a course suitable for a distance learning format; second, distance learners often require more individual, one-on-one attention, because questions that would normally be posed in a classroom, for all students to hear, may need to be addressed with each student individually. In addition, it generally takes longer to write a response than simply to reply to a question in person. Discussion boards and a frequently asked questions page, however, are two methods that faculty can use to save time. Requiring students to use these resources as much as possible not only benefits student learning but also reduces the time the instructor spends responding to individual e-mails.

Because faculty may be responsible for some course development, including content, structure, and technical components, they need to acquire and develop the new skills necessary to accomplish these tasks. This too inevitably increases their workload. Therefore, significant changes in institutional policies on monetary compensation, courseloads, and release time for distance learning faculty may be necessary.

Olcott and Wright (2002) discovered that departmental support—both monetary compensation and help in gaining needed skills—is crucial to the success of distance learning instructors. Yet most colleges that have programs to assist instructors with teaching at a distance are more focused on the technological aspects than on helping faculty adjust to their new role in an online environment. There remains a significant need for innovative faculty development that focuses on assisting online instructors in creating interactive individual and collaborative group activities (Van Dusen, 2002).

Content Organization and Format

The organization and format of content is a significant issue for faculty developing Web-based courses. Oliver (2002) estimated that online faculty spend almost 90 percent of their time on content development. Content itself, however, and especially online content, is not necessarily as important as the format in which it is presented. Community college faculty must consider organization, format, and delivery when transferring the content of their traditional courses to the online environment.

LaMonica (2001) surveyed online instructors and students and found that the most important element in a successful Web-based course was the organization of content. Both instructor and students indicated that Web-based content should be organized in an easy-to-follow manner. Whereas organizing content may be simple in a traditional course, organizing it so that it is readily understandable by a student who is not able to ask questions verbally can be a challenge.

Hoffman (2001) noted that the format of the Web obligates faculty to organize content more carefully and specifically than they would in a traditional classroom. For instance, overheads showing figures or tables must be transformed into slides, and supplemental information that would be verbally explained in the traditional classroom must be written out. The online format may even limit the presentation of information. For example, faculty who traditionally use videos in their courses are challenged to adapt to an online course format because students may not have the computer capability to view streaming video, or copyrights may limit presentation options.

There is also the issue of how to deliver the content. As in the face-to-face classroom, instructors can employ a number of alternative delivery methods online. However, it can be a challenge to find creative methods for delivering material in a manner that engages students. Programs such as Blackboard and WebCT offer a variety of methods by which students, faculty, and content can interact. For instance, students can build their own biographical Web pages as part of an introductory welcome activity. Instructors also can use discussion boards to invite guest speakers to share their experiences and expertise with students in online conversations.

Interaction and Communication

The nature of interaction in the online environment greatly affects how community college faculty teach their courses. In the traditional, face-to-face classroom, informal and spontaneous interactions often occur, and instructors are able to speak directly with students before, during, or after class. But in the online environment, faculty must plan for such interactions. Web-based courses are generally asynchronous, meaning that students can work at their own pace and do not necessarily have real-time interactions with the instructor. Though there may be synchronous elements of a course—such as real-time online chats—these are often limited. Because of the lack of verbal communication between faculty and students, e-mail is often one of the main forms of interaction. According to a study conducted by the National Education Association (2000), 83 percent of faculty teaching Web-based courses use e-mail as the dominant means of communicating with their students, and a significant number of these faculty never have face-to-face interaction with their students.

Moreover, body language and tone of voice do not exist in the online environment. Written communication may be interpreted in ways different than intended, and misinterpretation of statements can result in confusion and misunderstanding. Lynch (1998) emphasized the importance of communication in online learning and stressed that informal communication often better supports learning. Effective use of chat rooms, news groups, bulletin boards, and e-mail may help faculty improve the quality of communication and interaction with students.

Feedback can also be a significant concern for faculty and students in Web-based courses. LaMonica (2001) found that receiving timely and appropriate feedback was the second most important factor to students and faculty in the online environment. In a face-to-face course, feedback is often implicit—delivered through body language, eye contact, and physical interactions. For instance, faculty can assess whether students have understood instructions simply by looking around the classroom for signs of confusion or comprehension. And when a student physically hands an instructor an assignment, he or she knows that the teacher has received it. In contrast, in an online course, instructors must specifically plan how to judge students' comprehension of concepts and how to ensure effective transmission of information and assignments (Graham and others, 2001). Faculty must adjust their communication styles and be prompt in their replies to student inquiries. Procedures that are taken for granted in the traditional environment, such as receiving a student's assignment by hand, need to be properly adapted in order to allay student concerns.

Teaching and Assessment Methods

Research has shown that developing and teaching Web-based courses demands adaptations in teaching practices (Barr and Tagg, 1995). According to a national report, 83 percent of faculty and staff in postsecondary institutions use the lecture as their main instructional method (U.S. Department of Education, 2001). However, this method is not only difficult to use in the online environment but is clearly ineffective. Faculty who traditionally rely on lectures must find alternative methods to keep students engaged in their online courses. Interactive methods such as discussion groups and bulletin boards are increasingly being employed to engage students in these courses. Group projects that require students to work with one another can also enhance online course content. Thus, as already noted, technology not only has changed teaching methods but has actually transformed students' learning experiences. Community college faculty need to expand opportunities for student learning by moving from individual to group and team-oriented projects.

The use of technology increasingly implies a shift from a teaching to a learning paradigm (O'Banion, 1997). While classroom teaching is primarily verbal, visual technologies such as computers and television require students to shift from auditory learning to integrating both auditory and visual material. This shift creates many opportunities for students to use higher-level learning skills such as critical analysis and problem solving.

Assessment measures too must change in an online environment. Although 61 percent of traditional faculty members use competency-based assessments to grade their undergraduate classes (U.S. Department of Education, 2001), the traditional test is not always the best method in the online environment. Ensuring that a student is not receiving assistance with an exam, enforcing time limits, and adjusting to technical difficulties during an exam are all considerations when traditional tests are administered online. Each of these conditions is difficult, if not impossible, to monitor in the online environment. To supplement traditional exams, Fetherston (2001) identified alternative methods more appropriate to distance learning courses. For example, portfolios, individual or group projects, and ongoing participation in class discussion can help instructors evaluate student performance in distance learning courses while also encouraging learners to look at their experiences as part of a larger context, rather than simply as activities germane to the class at hand.

Copyright and Intellectual Property Issues

In addition to the preceding instructional and workload issues, issues of fair use and copyright are magnified in the online environment, as online content can be easily accessed and modified. Instructional supplements that would regularly be handed to students in a traditional class, or verbally delivered by the professor, cannot always be used online, where copyright infringement issues may arise. This is true not only with written materials but also with video clips, pictures, and other graphic or audio information gleaned from Web sites. Indeed, the complexity of copyright issues on the Web, and the resulting restrictions on course content, have made some instructors leery of becoming involved in online instruction.

This situation may be changing, however. In 2002 the national Technology, Education and Copyright Harmonization (TEACH) Act was passed, which clarified many of these copyright issues. Essentially, this act allows instructors to use copyrighted works in ways similar to those in the face-to-face classroom. That is, portions of material suitable for instructional purposes may be used as long as neither the entire work, nor lengthy portions of it, are copied. The act also stated that institutions, rather than individual instructors, are ultimately responsible for enforcing copyright (Crews, 2002).

Course ownership issues too often fall into a gray area. Although many institutions have recently worked with faculty to establish new guidelines for ownership of intellectual property, some have not done so or have encountered situations where their established guidelines do not apply. Course ownership can be ambiguous. The ease of determining ownership can vary depending on how involved various parties were in developing the course. On one end of the continuum, if a professor is not given institutional training or design support and develops the course primarily at home, he or she may have a strong claim to course ownership. On the other end of the continuum, if a professor depends in part on the assistance of others, including programmers and instructional designers, his or her claim for course ownership will not be as clear. In this case, the institution and several other individuals could also claim ownership.

The American Association of University Professors (1997) offers a report on distance education and intellectual property that addresses some of these issues. However, this report is simply a guideline for policy. It is up to community college administrators and faculty to work together to develop an official understanding of intellectual property specific to online courses and documents in order to avoid future disputes.

Conclusion

As this chapter has shown, community college faculty face a number of issues in a Web-based instructional environment, including changes in their role, workload, instruction and assessment methods, and how they handle intellectual property. All institutions that offer, or are considering offering, online courses must be mindful of these issues. In addition, community colleges should be aware of the profound organizational and pedagogical changes that accompany online courses. To facilitate a smooth transition, community colleges must put mechanisms in place to help faculty and administrators make the changes necessary to create successful distance learning environments and experiences for students.

References

American Association of Community Colleges. *The Knowledge Net: A Report of the New Expeditions Initiative.* Washington, D.C.: Community College Press, 2000.

American Association of University Professors. "Academic Freedom and Electronic Communications," 1997. http://www.aaup.org/statements/archives/reports/pre2000/Statelec.htm. Accessed Aug. 16, 2004.

Arreola, R. A. "Distance Education: The Emergence of America's Virtual University." In P. Seldin and Associates (eds.), *Improving College Teaching.* Bolton, Mass.: Anker, 1995.

Barr, R., and Tagg, J. "From Teaching to Learning: A New Paradigm for Undergraduate Education." *Change,* 1995, 2(5),13–25.

Crews, K. D. "New Copyright Law for Distance Education: The Meaning and Importance of the TEACH Act." Chicago: American Library Association, 2002. http://www.ala.org/ala/washoff/WOissues/copyrightb/distanceed/teachsummary.pdf. Accessed Oct. 4, 2004.

Dillon, C. L., and Walsh, S. M. "Faculty: The Neglected Resource in Distance Education." *American Journal of Distance Education,* 1992, 6(3), 5–21.

Fetherston, T. "Pedagogical Challenges for the World Wide Web." *Educational Technology Review,* 2001, 9(1). http://www.aace.org/pubs/etr/fetherston.cfm. Accessed Aug. 16, 2004.

Gillespie, F. "Instructional Design for the New Technologies." In K. H. Gillespie (ed.), *The Impact of Technology on Faculty Development, Life, and Work.* New Directions for Teaching and Learning, no. 76. San Francisco: Jossey-Bass, 1998.

Graham, C., and others. "Seven Principles of Effective Teaching: A Practical Lens for Evaluating Online Courses." *Technology Source,* Mar.-Apr. 2001.

Hoffman, R. "Technology's Impact on the Faculty: A Perspective." *Technology Source,* May-June 2001.

LaMonica, L. "The Role of the Instructor in Web-Based Instruction: Are We Practicing What We Preach?" *DEOSNEWS,* 2001, 11(6). http://www.geocities.com/llamonica/instructorwbt.html. Accessed Aug. 16, 2004.

Lynch, M. M. "Facilitating Knowledge Construction and Communication on the Internet." *Technology Source,* Dec. 1998.

Menges, R. "Teaching in the Age of Electronic Information." In W. J. McKeachie (ed.), *Teaching Tips: Strategies, Research, and Theory for College and University Teachers* (9th ed.). Lexington, Mass.: Heath, 1994.

National Education Association. *A Survey of Traditional and Distance Learning Higher Education Members.* Washington, D.C.: National Education Association, 2000.

O'Banion, T. *A Learning College for the 21st Century.* Phoenix: Oryx Press, 1997.

Olcott, Jr., D., and Wright, S. J. "An Institutional Support Framework for Increasing Faculty Participation in Postsecondary Distance Education." In L. Foster, B. L. Bower, and L. W. Watson (eds.), *ASHE Reader—Distance Education: Teaching and Learning in Higher Education* (pp. 285–291). Boston: Pearson Custom, 2002.

Oliver, R. "Exploring Strategies for Online Teaching and Learning." In L. Foster, B. L.

Bower, and L. W. Watson (eds.), *ASHE Reader—Distance Education: Teaching and Learning in Higher Education* (pp. 249–257). Boston: Pearson Custom, 2002.

Simonson, M., Smaldino, S., Albright, M., and Zvacek, S. *Teaching and Learning at a Distance: Foundations of Distance Education.* Upper Saddle River, N.J.: Prentice-Hall, 2000.

U.S. Department of Education, National Center for Education Statistics. *The Condition of Education, 2001* (NCES No. 2001–072). Washington, D.C.: U.S. Department of Education, 2001.

Van Dusen, G. C. "Teaching on the Virtual Campus: New Roles, New Responsibilities." In L. Foster, B. L. Bower, and L. W. Watson (eds.), *ASHE Reader—Distance Education: Teaching and Learning in Higher Education* (pp. 232–241). Boston: Pearson Custom, 2002.

Zukas, A. "Cyberworld: Teaching World History on the World Wide Web." *History Teacher,* 1999, 32, 495–516.

KIMBERLY P. HARDY *is a consultant for MGT of America, Inc., a national higher education research firm. She is a former community college administrator and has worked with the Florida Distance Learning Consortium.*

BEVERLY L. BOWER *is associate professor of higher education at Florida State University and a former community college administrator. She has taught using several distance education platforms and researches teaching and learning in distance education.*

7

This chapter describes exemplary community college student services programs and proposes a model designed to help community colleges reconfigure their support services for distance learners while also improving their services to on-campus students.

New Roles for Student Support Services in Distance Learning

Deborah L. Floyd, Deborah Casey-Powell

Although "student services [have] always played a major role in the two-year college" (Helfgot, 1995, p. 45), many students' physical time on campus has become virtually nonexistent as community colleges have expanded their distance learning programs. Hence, two-year colleges are challenged to find new ways to provide high-quality support services to both traditional and distance learners. This chapter discusses ways in which community colleges can strengthen the delivery of online courses to ensure that programs such as admissions, advising, and financial aid, as well as career and academic counseling, and library and registration services, are meeting the needs of distance learners. We rely on relevant research and literature in offering practical advice and ideas for research, policy, and implementation.

Characteristics of Successful Online Support Services

Successful online support services aid both students and faculty. As higher education expands its distance education offerings, "the diversity of its student population increases, particularly in the area of students' proficiency with technology" (Bruso, 2001, p. 9). This inequity in skill level can create problems for institutions that desire to provide sound support services for students taking online courses. What kind of tutorials, for example, should be developed to help students navigate online curricula? Do online student support services have the potential to be a great equalizer among students, or will they provide quality services only to those with access to the most current technology? These are just two of the myriad questions and issues that must be explored by colleges hoping to effectively support distance learners.

Research indicates that successful distance learners have a distinct profile. According to Seeman (2001), they possess self-discipline and self-confidence and have the ability to work independently and overcome frustration and confusion. In addition, successful online students must have access to required software and technological services. Yet providing access to technology for all students creates several challenges for community colleges, especially in light of the diverse clientele that most of them serve.

Colleges must also support faculty and create learning environments and campus cultures that support the teaching of online classes: "Successful distance learning institutions support their faculty who, in effect, become both students and users of the technology tools they will use to deliver the courseware" (RDR Associates, 1998, p. 17). Positive integration of student and faculty support, as well as the use of effective technology, encourage meaningful interaction between students and college professionals, and can provide a successful model for effective teaching and learning that helps to ensure student success.

Guidelines for Developing Effective Online Support Services

A plethora of literature describes successful online student support services. The term *student support services* refers to a variety of nonacademic interactions that the student has with a college or university (Dirr, 1999). These include preenrollment services (recruiting, promotion, and orientation), admissions and registration, academic advising, financial planning and management, library and bookstore services, academic and career counseling, social support services, degree and transcript auditing, and technical support.

Several organizations have published guidelines for institutions offering distance education. For example, a policy statement from the Southern Association of Colleges and Schools (2000) suggests that institutions offering distance education need to provide adequate access to an appropriate range of student support services, including admissions, financial aid, advising, delivery of course materials, and placement and counseling. Similarly, the Southern Regional Education Board (SREB) developed the *Principles of Good Practice for Electronically Offered Academic Degree and Certificate Programs* (2002–03), which lists specific program requirements for supporting distance learners. Bruce Chaloux describes these SREB principles in detail in Chapter Ten of this volume.

In addition to these guidelines, colleges can use a variety of tools to assess the support services they offer. One assessment tool, the Online Student Services Self-Assessment Tool (OLSS-SAT), helps users review college Web sites for important links and online services for students. It is an effective tool to use to evaluate existing support services and to identify new services that may still be needed.

Practices for Incorporating Online Student Services

Community colleges often lack the resources or flexibility to implement separate support services to meet the unique needs of the distance learner. However, it is not always necessary to develop new services for these students; often support already exists in other college units. For example, instructional faculty already provide much advising and technical support. Rather than implement a dual system of student affairs programming, which can be a fiscal burden, Floyd and Weihe (1985) propose that community college student support professionals serve as "catalytic partners" to design services that can be used by both traditional and distance students in order "to ensure that all students' needs are being met" (p. 128). As increasing numbers of students enroll in distance courses, a collaborative and efficient system of student services is essential.

The Learning Anytime Anyplace Partnership (LAAP), sponsored by the Fund for the Improvement of Postsecondary Education, offers an excellent model for incorporating existing student support services into distance learning programs. LAAP planners noted that most of the existing services on today's community college campus were designed from the institution's point of view, not that of the student. All too often, students are forced to go to various offices to receive support services—perhaps getting conflicting information and advice in the process. Students in the online environment often have the same experience; they may click from page to page and encounter conflicting information and advice. Instead, the LAAP's Project Web model offers a framework for planning, organizing, and delivering integrated student services designed from the student's point of view. Additional information about this model is available at http://www.wcet.info/projects/laap/guidelines/overview.asp.

Shea and Armitage (2003, n.p.) list several questions an institution should ask itself when incorporating online student support services:

> Are the services designed from the student's point of view, but tempered with the knowledge of the veteran staff? Are they seamlessly integrated, as appropriate? Are they interactive, providing real services online—not just information online about using available offline services? Do the services accommodate all users. . . . students, staff, and others as appropriate? Are the services flexible to accommodate customization by various departments or colleges? Will the services automate tasks to free staff to spend more time on personal services?

This list is not exhaustive, but it provides the important questions a student services support team should ask when thinking about designing new or adapting old services for online students.

A Model for Providing Inclusive Student Services

By implementing a systematic and inclusive approach to developing online student services, community colleges can encourage the collaborative involvement of the entire academic community. The systems framework we propose, the Inclusive Student Services Process Model, is based loosely on Miller and Prince's (1976) student development process model, which was intended to "meet the needs of all students, to plan for change rather than react to it, and to engage the full academic community in this collaborative effort" (p. 21). This new model provides a framework for designing processes and programs to support students in both traditional and online courses. Following phases of student matriculation, the model identifies five phases of student support services: learner intake, learner intervention, learner support, learner transition, and measurement of effectiveness (see Figure 7.1). The following sections describe these five phases in detail and suggest student support strategies that can be used at each phase by discussing exemplary online services at ten community colleges. The community college programs were selected using the OLSS-SAT assessment tool (Cox, 2001), and their Web sites were reviewed for user-friendliness.

Learner Intake Phase. Setting goals and assessing students' readiness for learning, including their desire and ability to engage in distance learning, are the key tasks during the learner intake phase. Student support services involved in this phase include admissions, preenrollment assessment, registration, financial aid, information technology, and orientation.

In order to support prospective online students, admissions and orientation information should be clearly stated on a college's homepage because it is critical to students' decision to enroll. Similarly, a user-friendly Web site that clearly differentiates between services for distance and on-campus learners is imperative. Adequate information on the admissions process, testing procedures, phone numbers, career planning opportunities, assessment tools, and online representatives should be provided to demonstrate the college's commitment to its online programs and services. Offering virtual or online orientation is an easy and convenient way to build rapport with distance learners, and is essential to ensuring successful enrollment and retention.

Several community colleges have effectively implemented online admissions and orientation services. For example, Colorado Community Colleges Online (http://www.ccconline.org) has a virtual admissions representative who is available to answer questions, accept applications, and complete orientation. In addition, a link on the Web site allows students to take self-assessments to determine if distance learning is the right modality for them. Similarly, Pitt Community College's (North Carolina) Web site (http://www. pitt.cc.nc.us) offers distance learners a tutorial and a quiz to help explain how online instruction works at the college. As well, Houston Community College (Texas; http://www.hccs.edu) places the

Figure 7.1. Inclusive Student Services Process Model

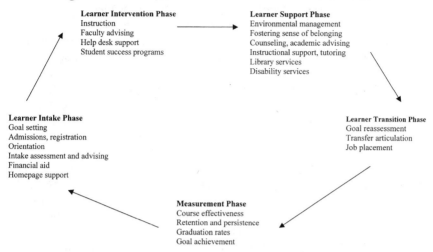

student handbook online so students can read the code of conduct, find resources on campus, and learn about other student support services. Pitt Community College and Houston Community College also post links to their course catalogues and academic calendars.

Online support services for students seeking financial aid should be clear and concise and include deadlines for applications, fee schedules and payment options, and links to scholarships, government loans, and other loan sites. The Web site should also include a link to the Free Application for Federal Student Aid (http://www.fafsa.ed.gov). Pitt Community College and Bellevue Community College (Washington; http://www.bcc.ctc.edu) both offer links to scholarship and federal financial aid resources on their Web sites. These links provide valuable information on available financial resources as well as on procedures for applying for and receiving financial aid.

Community college Web sites should also clearly describe and explain the registration process, schedule, and policies. As well, students should be able to find out how to add or drop a course, check grades, verify tuition owed, and access course schedules through the registration Web site. Brevard Community College (Florida; http://web2010.brevard.cc.fl.us) and Bellevue Community College both give students online access to course schedules, registration procedures, grades, and transcripts.

Learner Intervention Phase. Online courses are delivered during the second phase of the model, learner intervention. The primary goal during this phase is to assist students in self-development and independent learning. Support strategies offered in this phase include instruction on student success strategies, student help desk support, technology training, and online faculty advising. Faculty advisers and help desk support are integral to ensuring student success in the learner intervention phase.

Rio Salado College in Arizona, for example, offers distance learners ample resources in support of traditional and online academic services. Rio Salado offers a technology help desk and "Successful Start Workshops," and its Web site (http://www.rio.maricopa.edu) provides links to problem-solving resources. The site also includes a link to a "suggestion box," where students can deposit ideas for making the Web site more user-friendly.

Effective community college Web sites also provide technology training to both students and faculty. Rio Salado College's Web site links to a training site for adjunct faculty. Similarly, Brevard Community College's site provides links to tools for faculty and students, and to a help desk that can assist the online user.

Learner Support Phase. During the learner support phase, students learn self-development strategies so that they can accept responsibility for developing their own skills. Key support services during this phase are academic advising, instructional support and tutoring, library and bookstore services, disability services, and networking.

Community colleges offering distance learning courses must provide effective online advising, tutoring, and testing to assist students with course selection and placement. Professional advice is critical in helping students meet their degree or certificate objectives, and students must be placed in the correct course levels if they are to succeed academically. Student services during the learner support phase must offer study tips, test-taking tips, and external instructional resources such as tutoring; also important is providing reasonable accommodations to distance learning students with disabilities, and designing Web sites with links to information about articulation and transferring credits.

Rio Salado College's advising program for distance learners is exceptional. Its Web site offers students the opportunity to e-mail questions, seek tutoring, transfer courses, determine prerequisites, and join a chat room. Similarly, Bunker Hill Community College (Massachusetts; http://www.bhcc.edu) links students to an external tutoring service and facilitates e-mail communication with advisers. Portland Community College (Oregon; http://www.pcc.edu) has developed online writing labs as well as a College Survival Success course, and the Community College of Baltimore (Maryland; http://www.ccbcmd.edu) offers cybertutoring. As well, Colorado Community Colleges Online has developed clear policies for online students with disabilities that are consistent with other college disability service protocols and provide an inclusive environment for distance learning students with disabilities.

Most online libraries offer students links to full-text databases, electronic books, journals, and the college's online library catalogue. Distance learners today expect remote access to these services. The most effective community college Web sites offer library services as a direct link from the college's homepage. Online library orientations, e-mail access to librarians, and online tutorials on how to conduct Web research help distance learners succeed.

Learner Transition Phase. During the learner transition phase students need career, transfer, counseling, and job placement services. To be successful in this phase, community colleges must work collaboratively to coordinate resources and design programs that assist students in their personal and professional transitions. Career development and counseling services are key during this phase; helping students to build their professional resumes, develop interviewing strategies, and deal with life issues, are instrumental in retaining students.

Portland Community College has excellent career and counseling services for distance learners. Students can take a variety of courses focused on career development, such as a ten-week course that covers occupational information, interviews, decision making, and goal setting. Similarly, Rio Salado College offers distance learners a self-assessment tool to help determine their interests, locate job market information, and find information on educational requirements for specific jobs. In addition, personal development and resume writing tips can be found on its Web site. Houston Community College has counselors available specifically to address mental health issues and disability accommodations for distance learners.

Measurement Phase. The final phase of the model focuses on evaluating the effectiveness of a college's online programs and delivery systems. In this phase, colleges should assess retention, graduation, and persistence rates, and they should review online course evaluations. This phase is important because it ensures that institutions focus on accountability and use feedback about student services programs in order to continually improve.

Taken together, these five phases of the Inclusive Student Services Process Model provide a systems approach to supporting online students in meaningful ways, regardless of campus location or instructional delivery system. The model relies on traditional methods of student support services, and challenges professionals to create new paradigms for ensuring distance learning student success. However, each individual college needs to refine the model to meet its specific needs. The most important point is that the student comes first: all programs and services should be designed and implemented with student success as the primary goal.

Two advantages of this model are that it provides support for students from matriculation through graduation and it emphasizes student success. This multidimensional model benefits all students while also demonstrating a college's commitment to the success of distance learners.

Recommendations

The key to implementing successful student support services for distance learners in the twenty-first century is for faculty and staff to pragmatically and systematically redefine traditional student support services to ensure success for all learners. Traditional services such as admissions, advising, registration, financial aid, career services, counseling, and library services must be reframed to incorporate strategies that meet the needs of a techno-logically oriented student population. This effort requires all campus constituents to work collaboratively toward student success, regardless of the instructional delivery system.

To tackle the challenges of reframing and implementing distance education support services, administrators and student service educators may want to consider the following recommendations.

• First, community colleges must develop a process model for student support services that measures the effectiveness of programs and services for all types of students. All support services must be designed and implemented around a commitment to the learner, regardless of delivery system. This may appear fundamental, yet most student services are geared toward the traditional rather than the distance learner.

• Second, colleges must realign their priorities and redesign how student services are delivered to ensure consistency with the institution's commitment to offer online courses and degrees. Distance learners should have access to the same resources as on-campus students. To accomplish this, student service educators need to redefine their roles, as faculty have done, to accommodate distance learners.

• Third, changing student support services to incorporate distance learners requires professional development and in-service training. A community college counselor who has worked primarily on campus, for example, may feel uncomfortable working with students online. Such feelings can be addressed, along with technical issues, during in-service training. In-service training can also help student service educators better understand the distance learner population and learn current theories and intervention strategies for this group of students.

• Fourth, to be effective, distance learning support services must be integrated into a college's mainstream activities. Although most campus Web sites include links to such essential information as applications, registration, and course catalogues, many still do not provide interactive links to all services.

• Finally, an institution's funding priorities must be aligned with their commitment to distance learning student success. Community colleges must commit financial resources to develop technology for student services. Technology should be budgeted as a fixed cost, similar to electricity and insurance, and colleges should fund distance learning support services as an integral part of the institution.

Conclusion

Distance learning students expect to receive online support services that will allow them to succeed in their educational endeavors. Moreover, they are willing to shop around for institutions that can offer the services and learning experiences they want. Without question, online support services must be user-friendly and learner-centered. This is an extension of the basic community college philosophy and student services mission.

Distance learners expect student support services to accommodate them from their point of entry (learner intake) through completion of their certificate or degree (learner transition). They expect rapid responses to requests for advising, career and academic counseling services, and library resources (learner intervention and support). As Dalziel and Payne (2001) note, "Providing effective, efficient online student services is an enormous challenge for higher education administrators" (p. 5). Yet doing so is necessary if community college educators are to honor their commitment to student success by enhancing support services for all constituents.

Enrollment in online programs and courses is rapidly increasing. Yet retaining these students will become problematic if community college administrators do not commit to maintaining appropriate support services for this progressive population. Distance learners dissatisfied with one college's online support services will simply enroll elsewhere. Thus, student support services must be redefined and implemented systematically, and they must be continually evaluated to ensure satisfaction and success among all students.

References

Bruso, J. L. "A Comprehensive Orientation to Address Diverse Student Needs." In C. Dalziel and M. Payne (eds.), *Quality Enhancing Practices in Distance Education: Student Services.* Washington, D.C.: Instructional Telecommunications Council, 2001.

Cox, D. H. *Online Student Services Self-Assessment Tool.* Unpublished paper adapted from the Western Cooperative for Educational Telecommunications' "Online Student Services Provision: A Guide for Good Practice" and the Council for the Advancement of Standards and Guidelines, 2001. http://irt.austincc.edu/presentations/2003/aacc/McRaeOnlineStudentServices.pdf. Accessed Aug. 16, 2004.

Dalziel, C., and Payne, M. (eds.). *Quality Enhancing Practices in Distance Education: Student Services.* Washington, D.C.: Instructional Telecommunications Council, 2001.

Dirr, P. J. *Putting Principles into Practice: Promoting Effective Support Services for Students in Distance Learning Programs: A Report on the Findings of a Survey.* Project report funded by the U.S. Department of Education's Fund for the Improvement of Postsecondary Education, 1999. http://www.wcet.info/projects/studentservices. Accessed Aug. 17, 2004.

Floyd, D. L., and Weihe, L. "Commitments to Non-Credit Students: Issues for Student Development Educators." *Journal of Staff Program and Organization Development,* 1985, 3(4), 128–132.

Helfgot, S. R. "Counseling at the Center: High Tech, High Touch." In S. R. Helfgot and M. G. Culp (eds.), *Promoting Student Success in the Community College.* New Directions for Student Services, no. 69. San Francisco: Jossey-Bass, 1995.

Miller, T., and Prince, J. *The Future of Student Affairs. A Guide to Student Development for Tomorrow's Higher Education.* San Francisco: Jossey-Bass, 1976.

RDR Associates. *New Connections: A Guide to Distance Education.* Washington, D.C.: Instructional Telecommunications Council, 1998.

Seeman, E. "Creating an Online Orientation and Student Support Services." In C. Dalziel and M. Payne (eds.), *Quality Enhancing Practices in Distance Education: Student Services*. Washington, D.C.: Instructional Telecommunications Council, 2001.

Shea, P., and Armitage, S. "Guidelines for Creating Student Services Online." In P. Shea and S. Armitage (eds.), *WCET LAAP Project Beyond the Administrative Core: Creating Web-Based Student Services for Online Learners*. Boulder, Colo.: Western Cooperative for Educational Technologies, 2003. http://www.wcet.info/projects/laap/guidelines/overview.htm. Accessed Aug. 16, 2004.

Southern Association of Colleges and Schools, Commission on Colleges. *Distance Education: Definition and Principles: A Policy Statement*. Atlanta: Southern Association of Colleges and Schools, 2000.

Southern Regional Education Board. *Principles of Good Practice: The Foundation for Quality of the Electronic Campus*. Atlanta: Southern Regional Education Board, 2002–03.

DEBORAH L. FLOYD is an associate professor of higher education leadership at Florida Atlantic University in Boca Raton. She has also been a community college dean, vice president of student affairs, and community college president.

DEBORAH CASEY-POWELL is director of student affairs for the Honors College at Florida Atlantic University. She was previously dean of student affairs at South University and has worked in housing and student life as well as in student activities at Holyoke Community College.

8

This chapter recounts Oregon community colleges'
challenges and successes in developing a statewide
distance learning consortium.

Oregon's Seventeen-Member Statewide Distance Learning Collaborative

Cynthia R. Andrews

Rapid and wide-ranging changes in the ways Oregonians live, work, and learn provided impetus for a distance learning partnership between the community colleges, the Oregon Department of Education (ODE), and the Office of Community Colleges and Workforce Development (OCCWD). This collaboration has remained flexible, responsive, and economically sustainable despite the many organizational and budgetary challenges it has faced, and has provided expanded access to quality education and training.

The complex structure of the state's community college system has had a significant impact on the development and organization of Oregon's statewide distance learning consortium. The state has seventeen independent community colleges, each governed by a separate board of education that is elected by voters in each college's district. Each community college has its own president and sets its own internal governance policies, budget, salaries, operating procedures, curriculum, and programs in accordance with the policies and guidelines set forth by the OCCWD. Most of the community colleges are affiliated with the Oregon Education Association and have individually negotiated faculty and support staff contracts. These unique contracts spell out many of the details regarding workload, compensation, course development, technology use, intellectual property ownership, and other instructional and support issues that affect distance learning at both local and state levels.

Collaboration under this decentralized, independent, and sometimes very competitive structure is challenging. In addition, budget shortfalls over several years have seriously affected available resources for course development, distribution, support infrastructure, staffing, and technology, both locally and statewide. Because of these organizational and financial challenges, Oregon's distance learning agreement had to take into consideration the educational practices and philosophies of individual communities and local boards; organizational, financial, and curricular differences among colleges; and unique staff contracts. The proverbial phrase "herding cats" is an apt analogy for this process. Nevertheless, Oregon's experience, as detailed in this chapter, may be useful to other states and community college systems attempting to develop successful distance learning consortiums.

A Brief History

The Oregon Community College Telecommunications Consortium (OCCTC) was formed in 1981 with support from Oregon community college presidents and through grassroots efforts by distance learning practitioners in several community colleges. Many of this organization's concepts, agreements, and practices provided a foundation for future statewide community college distance learning collaborations and resource sharing. Distance learning in Oregon in the early 1980s consisted primarily of telecourses, although correspondence, videotaped, and two-way interactive courses were also available. OCCTC focused on distance learning coordination, collaborative course distribution, group licensing negotiation, and telecourse cost sharing. Membership in OCCTC was optional, but a founding principle was that all community college members would participate "for the greater good." That is, decision making would be shared, and no college would leverage decisions exclusively for its own benefit.

The consortium was funded by the colleges' general fund budgets; each college contributed annual fees, which were then pooled for consortium use. OCCTC obtained nonprofit status, maintained its own fund account, and was advised by an independent accountant. Each president designated one distance learning practitioner or manager to be a representative, and another to be an alternate. Although representatives were charged to provide two-way communication between OCCTC and their respective colleges, they were also challenged to think both statewide and locally. Because representatives came from large, small, rural, and urban institutions where they served as administrators, technology professionals, academic managers, and technicians, the organization had great vitality, diversity, and strength. At OCCTC all were equal partners. As the organization grew in complexity and scope, the consortium hired a part-time administrative assistant to manage college and agency agreements, partnerships, licensing, technology agreements and contracts, and budget and tax forms and to facilitate communication between colleges. All members benefited from the cost-saving agreements that OCCTC was able to broker.

Throughout the 1980s and 1990s, the organization remained responsive to the changing nature of education and distance learning. In 1995, however, acknowledging changes in delivery technology, the impact of the

Internet, virtual universities, and an increasing community college population that included students with needs for more flexible access and program delivery, the organization changed both its name and its focus to become the Oregon Community College Distance Education Consortium (OCCDEC). As the development and delivery of online courses became the new thrust, the organization eventually developed two arms: Oregon Community Colleges Online (OCCOL), charged with the operational aspects of the consortium, and the Distance Learning Council, responsible for strategic planning and implementation of collaborative efforts. OCCOL is now subcontracted to one of the community colleges, and is funded by the state through OCCWD. The Distance Learning Council, however, remains a collaborative body with representatives appointed by individual community college presidents. Council members volunteer their time, and either the organization or the local college picks up travel expenses for quarterly meetings. For governance purposes, the consortium developed articles of agreement that spell out the conduct of its business.

Oregon's Distance Learning Strategic Plan

In 1996, budget shortfalls and a shortage of classroom space, as well as a rapidly growing community college student population, further stimulated the interest of the legislature, the academic community, and the public in distance learning. These conditions, coupled with increased competition from private and proprietary schools, prompted community college presidents and the OCCWD to support the development of a comprehensive strategic plan and infrastructure for expanded statewide community college collaboration on distance learning programs and services. The purpose of the *Strategic Plan of the Oregon Community Colleges for Distance Learning* (SPOCCDL) was to establish a common vision, to define strategic directions, and to identify implementation strategies for the coordinated delivery of distance learning services throughout the network of Oregon community colleges.

An eighteen-member SPOCCDL planning advisory committee, including seventeen representatives from the community colleges and OCCWD and led by a newly hired director of distance learning, created a strategic plan that was broad in scope yet flexible enough to allow individual colleges to tailor the application to their own particular infrastructure. The plan consisted of four key components: centralized clerical and administrative support, the host-provider network, shared revenue costs and full-time equivalency (FTE) reimbursement, and shared leadership, vision, and planning. These four components continue to be important issues for effective statewide collaboration.

Specific responsibilities were detailed for providers, hosts, the state, and the operational arm of the consortium with respect to marketing, instruction, course textbooks and materials, student course information, and FTE tuition reimbursement. It also specified practices related to student services, technology requirements or options, and student support. Additional start-up funding for the project was important, and the new director and college presidents were instrumental in successfully seeking the allocation of these funds from the legislature. Once state funds were allocated, contributions by the individual colleges ceased, and state money was used in the development of the collaborative and for operational support. Later, other state funds were granted to the colleges for extensive development of online curriculum that was to be shared under host-provider agreements.

The Host-Provider Framework

Host-provider agreements facilitate the sharing of curriculum between institutions. In a host-provider framework, the provider college funds the development, instruction, and delivery of distance learning courses, and then shares them or makes them available to other community colleges in the state. Students can then enroll in any distance learning class offered by any of the community colleges without paying out-of-district tuition.

To begin the process, the provider college selects which of its distance offerings, if any, it wants to make available to host schools in any particular term. The provider also determines how many virtual seats it will make available to students at host colleges. The host college then enters into an operational agreement to offer provider courses as part of its curriculum. Optimally, this is all accomplished in a timely manner so the host college can select the courses it needs or wants in time to publish the information in its course bulletin, and so it can provide advising, registration, financial aid, and other related student services. It is ideal if the provider school can develop an annual schedule of classes available under the agreement, but this is not always possible or practical.

The host school adds the selected courses to its own term schedule, and for all practical purposes, treats the hosted course like one of its own. Although the class is clearly identified to the student as a hosted class, students can register for it at their home college, following regular enrollment processes. Financial aid for distance learning can be used according to the home college policy, and credit for hosted classes counts the same as resident credit for the purposes of financial aid, academic eligibility, and transcripts. Students receive their end-of-term grades from their home college in the usual manner. Stipulations set forth in the SPOCCDL regulate the handling of exams and final course grades, and both provider and host colleges cooperate in matters related to enrollment, assessment, and admission, making the entire process smooth and nearly transparent for the student.

Information about distance learning courses is offered on individual colleges' distance learning homepages. Many of these Web sites are quite extensive, offering not only course information but also self-assessment, online technology training in local distance learning software, tips for negotiating the online environment, and time management and study tips. An OCCOL operation also maintains a central Web site (http://oregoncollegesonline. com) that contains course availability and other pertinent information for students, as well as an administrative site for participating colleges. This site lists all available community college online courses, not just those available through host-provider agreements.

Although they vary throughout the year, a full range of provider courses, from art to winemaking, are offered to students. Courses include those needed to transfer to a four-year university, basic skills, counseling and guidance, and professional or technical training. Courses must meet all pertinent state and regional accreditation requirements, and must reflect internal provider quality indicators. Accreditation requirements also ensure that each course incorporates a high degree of participant interactivity.

There are many benefits to students, colleges, and the state under a host-provider agreement. Students enjoy greater access to a wide variety of courses, flexibility in meeting degree and program requirements, and the ability to use financial aid for classes not available at their home colleges. As well, the host college provides learners with student services, financial aid, and library assistance. Provider colleges benefit because they can pilot new curricula to an expanded market and thereby recover some of the costs of development and instruction. In addition, students from other colleges can bolster enrollment in advanced or unusual courses. Finally, such courses may serve as marketing devices, encouraging students to explore other courses and curricula at the provider institution.

Host colleges benefit from a host-provider agreement as well, because they are able to offer courses to their students that might otherwise be unavailable. There is also some cost recovery for services rendered, but perhaps more importantly, the host school maintains a relationship with the local student who is enrolling in distance classes. The state benefits because new programs and curricula are developed at a relatively low cost, because innovation can be economically and readily shared, and because program duplication can be reduced. Online programs do not generally require new facilities, and with this type of collaboration between colleges, a greater number of citizens are provided with easier, more flexible access to higher education and training.

Revenue Sharing and Its Challenges

Under Oregon's original host-provider agreement, revenues from host student tuition and FTE were shared equally between the host and provider, and the enrolling college kept college-specific fees. FTE and tuition reimbursement were based on statewide averages as computed by OCCWD. The operations arm of OCCOL developed a quarterly billing method for participating colleges. Most colleges charged a special distance learning fee in addition to the usual tuition. If additional course-specific fees were attached to a course by the provider college, they were collected as a part of the institutional billing process.

However, in many cases, it took OCCWD two or more years to reimburse institutions for their FTE distance enrollments. When the reimbursements did come in, they usually went directly into the college's general fund, and individual distance learning or academic departments at the provider colleges never recovered their costs for distance learning development and operations. Therefore, the revenue sharing method led to general dissatisfaction with the host-provider agreement, and college participation fell dramatically in 2002 and 2003. Today, only a small percentage of approximately thirty-three thousand online students are enrolled in host-provider classes, although overall participation in distance learning has risen sharply.

Enrollment growth was another problematic factor in the original host-provider agreement. Once distance learning gained popularity, provider colleges were able to fill their classes with their own students, for which they received 100 percent of the tuition and FTE, instead of the 50 percent they earned by enrolling students from host colleges. In short, there was no financial incentive for most providers to keep participating. The few colleges that continued to participate decided to limit enrollment to only a few hosted students per section. Because they failed to provide adequate support for participants, Oregon's distance learning consortium was no longer able to provide the access envisioned when the host-provider framework was created.

Therefore, a new reimbursement plan was developed in 2002 and 2003 that included an annual cash FTE reimbursement from OCCWD directly to the institutions, and a more balanced approach to program tuition reimbursement. Unfortunately, however, the initial enthusiasm and commitment to statewide course sharing have not recovered. Only a handful of colleges now serve as providers, and some have negotiated their own host-provider agreements outside of the consortium. There have been some attempts at additional collaborative course development and delivery, but they have not been entirely successful. Differing technologies, instructional practices, pay scales, and annual academic calendars create many barriers. It is clear that Oregon must reexamine the host-provider aspect of its statewide collaboration, and find a way to remove barriers and provide additional incentives if this structure is to continue to play an important role in statewide distance learning. Continuing budget shortfalls at the state and local levels, however, make this a tremendous challenge.

Administrative Leadership, Governance, and Change

The importance of leadership and practitioner participation in a successful statewide consortium cannot be overemphasized. The consortium's function and goals must be understood and supported by college presidents, and the role of a state-level leader must be clearly defined. The

Oregon consortium operates most effectively when these goals and roles are clearly understood, and it is thus better able to achieve positive outcomes for the colleges and their students. Positive results are also achieved when both operations and planning components work closely together and are guided by a variety of distance learning professionals at all of the colleges. In addition, Oregon has learned that the practical and specific duties of the consortium's operations arm must be clearly spelled out, that the role of the Distance Learning Council (the strategic planning arm) must be carefully articulated, and that the consortium's relationship to OCCWD and the state director of distance learning must be clearly understood by all parties.

As Oregon's distance learning consortium has changed over the years, clarity of leadership roles has been a recurrent challenge. Between 1999 and 2001, the relationship between the state distance learning director and the council of college presidents was ambiguous, thus hampering effective leadership. During this same period, the operations and planning arms were quite separate, did not communicate clearly, and did not understand one another's needs and goals. In addition, between 1999 and 2001 the Distance Learning Council was separate from consortium representatives and was primarily made up of administrators from a variety of stakeholder groups who reported directly to the state distance learning director. These administrators were not always familiar with distance learning trends, student needs, emerging technologies, local practices, or the pragmatic details of operations. Communication broke down, and the planning and implementation of new practices, licensing agreements, and other sharing endeavors critical to the statewide effort languished.

The current model that was developed in 2001 and 2002, however, provides for a representative Distance Learning Council appointed by the college presidents, which has broad oversight over both operations and strategic planning. The representatives come from a variety of distance learning–related institutional roles, and they understand both the operations and planning needs of their institutions. The consortium's operations arm maintains its own organization, but meets regularly with the council.

The current model also eliminated the position of state director of distance learning. Since then, distance learning is no longer as visible as it once was to the state legislature and other statewide administrative bodies. OCCWD and the Distance Learning Council are discussing this problem and strategizing how the role of the position might be addressed under existing budget constraints. A strong leader with high visibility and a clear charge for strategic planning is important in seeking legislative and grant funds, developing additional infrastructure, and implementing shared vision and goals to move the state to a new level of collaborative effort. Only innovative collaboration based on today's realities can achieve a distance learning environment that meets the needs of Oregon's colleges and its diverse students.

Conclusion

Oregon's experience with a statewide community college distance learning consortium can be seen as both a guide and a cautionary tale for others interested in creating distance learning collaborations. As Oregon learned, a good statewide distance learning organization alone does not guarantee a successful outcome. The plan must be supported by strong commitments at both the state and local levels, must have clear leadership and communication, and must be carried out by a diverse group of individuals who understand the practical results and effects of decisions made in the statewide planning process. Such a plan must be flexible enough to keep pace with changes in distance learning, and must ensure that consortium membership has advantages commensurate with the demands of participation, especially when resources are tight.

By their very nature, voluntary agreements like the OCCDEC depend on each member's evaluation of the costs and benefits of participation. It takes leadership with vision, good communication, appropriate incentives, and a well-designed strategic plan to develop and maintain such a consortium. The Oregon community college system has learned how to collaborate to provide quality distance learning opportunities for its citizens; the challenge now is to rebuild relationships and reconfigure its strategic plan for future initiatives.

CYNTHIA R. ANDREWS is interim chair of Oregon Community Colleges Online and the Oregon Community Colleges Distance Learning Consortia. She is also director of the Learning Resource Center at Clackamas Community College.

9

Community colleges face a variety of challenges as they seek to expand innovative and effective uses of technology. This chapter discusses questions that must be answered as colleges move into the next phase of distance education.

Meeting the Next Phase of Challenges

Lenoar Foster

To accommodate an ever-larger and more diverse community of students and prepare them to meet the new workforce demands, community colleges have employed a vast array of technological innovations in online instruction and administrative support. These innovations, however, have also stretched infrastructures and resources, and in some cases, complicated community colleges' ability to meet their traditional educational objectives. Ultimately, community colleges will need to ask how these technological innovations can be sustained, and how resources devoted to technology might also be aligned with their traditional missions of transfer, community service, vocational-technical training, and continuing and developmental education. The next phase in the expansion of technology infrastructure and online education at the nation's community colleges is fraught with challenges and problems, but it also promises opportunities for expanding educational access.

The next phase will require answers to the following questions: What are the current and effective uses of technology in community colleges, and how are these uses tied to institutional mission, access, teaching and learning, and cost? What roles do faculty members see for themselves as technology becomes more widely used? What factors might inhibit student access to the community college during the next phase of technology integration? How might mixed-mode or hybrid courses affect teaching and learning and cost-effectiveness? What institutional strategies hold the greatest promise for meeting the challenges of the next phase of online education and the demands of a new workforce? Ultimately, these questions help to define the core activities that community college administrators and faculty

NEW DIRECTIONS FOR COMMUNITY COLLEGES, no. 128, Winter 2004 © Wiley Periodicals, Inc.

must carry out in order to begin the next phase of technology integration. This chapter examines each of these important questions in detail and suggests possible future directions and innovations.

Technology, Institutional Mission, and Cost

Technology transforms the teaching and learning process, providing community college faculty with unique opportunities to promote student-centered interaction and monitor and evaluate student progress (Bates and Poole, 2003; Doucette, 1994; McKinney, 1996). Online courses can be custom made for remedial, regular, and advanced students, and are accessible at a variety of on- and off-campus sites. For example, by using multimedia technology, "instructors can create attention-catching lectures and can also generate plans which allow them to change format based on student learning and interest" (Miketta and Ludford, quoted in McKinney, 1996, p. 3). Two course-authoring programs that currently dominate the development of online courses and have made it possible to create student-oriented, interactive online activities are WebCT and Blackboard. Technological applications allow for the integration of specific text material, sound bites, full-motion video clips, photographs, and other graphics that promote instructor creativity and facilitate active student engagement in the learning process. Thus online courses provide greater access for students, especially those who are limited by time and place. As well, online discussion techniques enable faculty to create a forum in which reclusive or shy students may be more comfortable voicing their views than in a traditional classroom. The Internet can connect students with local, regional, state, national, and international communities, and it provides a new means of fostering student diversity at the community college.

But although community colleges have invested heavily in technology and provided greater access to programs, many technical infrastructures are currently at risk because colleges must grapple with tight budgets and increasing numbers of students with diverse educational needs, as well as the need for workforce training and retraining (Young, 2004). More important, the cost of building and sustaining a viable technological infrastructure challenges community colleges to maintain their mission of providing open access to all students. No one doubts that technology integration has benefited community college policies, procedures, and practices. Yet it is also clear that community colleges must think about the costs of acquiring and maintaining a new technological infrastructure as well as how those costs affect the rest of the college. As Jacobs (1995) noted, computers become outdated six years after purchase, and upgrades are generally required three years after purchase. Meanwhile, increases in the number of students, faculty, and staff require comparable investments in computer systems. Updating computer software applications and replacing or updating peripherals are also costs that must be met if community colleges are to prepare students for placement in new and growing industries. Because most community colleges cannot afford to be state of the art, they must think carefully about how technology affects both their institutional mission and costs.

Faculty Roles

Community college faculty often hold divergent views about distance education. For some, distance education provides the excitement of being pioneers in linking the needs of diverse learners with the increasing academic and economic demands of their communities. But other community college faculty fear that colleges will fund technology over personnel during institutional restructuring. Because distance education may allow community colleges to teach a greater number of students with fewer faculty, some worry that increasing technology expenditures might be an attractive way for administrators to justify reducing faculty ranks and salaries.

Indeed, some studies indicate that when institutions align courses and change teaching methods to incorporate technology more effectively, they may in fact be able to support quality curricula while reducing faculty (Bates and Poole, 2003; Schifter, 2002; Van Dusen, 2002). However, research overwhelmingly shows that technology is most effective when it is complemented by a knowledgeable instructor (Bates and Poole, 2003; Biner, Bink, Huffman, and Dean, 2002; Palloff and Pratt, 2002a, 2002b). Thus, while instructors' fears are valid, they should work with administrators to create opportunities, rather than risks, in the next phase of technology implementation and integration.

Student Access

Providing universal student access may prove to be difficult as enrollments increase and state budgets diminish. Despite the increased flexibility technology brings, some students—especially those limited by location or finances—may not have access to the equipment or services they need to participate in distance learning programs. Thus, the next phase of technology integration may foster an inequitable system that benefits some students but excludes others, creating an uneven playing field for educational advancement and contradicting the community college's primary mission. Chapter Four discusses access issues in more detail.

Hybrid Courses

One of the unexpected phenomena growing out of the increasing use of the Internet is the integration of distance and face-to-face education. Hybrid course designs are also known as *mixed mode, distributed learning,* or *blended teaching* (Bates and Poole, 2003). A hybrid class might meet face-to-face once a week, and require students to spend the rest of their time interacting online. Or the course might be delivered in the traditional, face-to-face manner but use the Web to enhance teaching and learning through incorporation of online assignments and exercises. Other examples of hybrid or mixed-mode formats include redesigning lectures to incorporate technology-based programs, identifying teaching materials that can be universally applied across the curriculum, simulating laboratory experiments online to help students make more efficient use of their real-time lab experiences, designing core content that can be used to provide uniform instruction, and using technology to provide multiple ways of learning subjects that students find particularly challenging.

Community colleges are fertile ground for hybrid courses because of the varied academic levels and learning styles of the student clientele they serve. According to Bates and Poole (2003), hybrid course models present a variety of cost-effective options for institutions struggling with the challenges of restrained budgets and bulging student enrollments.

Promising Institutional Strategies

By investing in technology, community colleges can make their educational services more flexible and accessible to students. However, integrating technology into community college teaching and learning requires considerable investments of financial and human resources. Fortunately, several promising strategies exist to guide colleges interested in expanding their technological capabilities.

Perform Technology Audits. Each community college's ongoing strategic plan should include a technology audit that identifies existing technological conditions and infrastructure requirements. Creating audit committees at the institutional and programmatic levels is essential to this process. At the institutional level, committees conduct research and produce reports that outline the institution's infrastructure needs. These reports can help administrators choose the technological applications that will best meet institutional needs and eliminate waste and duplication. At the programmatic level, committees outline the essential functions and tasks necessary to deliver high-demand programs, and then precisely describe the type of equipment and tools that will be needed to accomplish this. Technology audits can be helpful in creating a three-to-five year plan for positioning institutional resources to renew and rejuvenate programs and provide for faculty and staff professional development.

Expand Institutional Partnerships. In addition to performing technology audits, community colleges interested in capitalizing on technology must expand institutional partnerships. As already noted, computer technology is constantly evolving, and those changes can be costly for educational institutions. Yet community colleges must stay current and provide students with technology skills that can be quickly and effectively applied in the workplace. In many instances, nearby companies have already invested in the computer technology necessary to serve their own needs; community colleges can create partnerships with these corporations to expose students to the types of technology used in the workplace. Coordinating academic and internship offerings not only helps students make the transition to the workplace but also reduces the burden on community colleges to purchase state-of-the-art equipment. In addition, such coordination gives community college faculty an opportunity to work closely with practitioners who can help them understand the skills students will need in the workplace.

Partnerships with companies that manufacture and distribute the hardware and software students will use when they enter the workforce are also desirable. Such partnerships not only provide corporations with opportunities to test and pilot their products, but also establish a ready cadre of employable recruits. And again, when community colleges collaborate with nearby businesses, they reduce technological infrastructure expenditures.

Market Online Educational Services. There is a great need for online academic and professional courses, and community colleges can tap into this valuable source of additional funding by marketing their online educational programs and services to surrounding communities and nearby organizations. Community colleges must begin to view themselves as viable brokers of the educational alternatives and services they can provide.

Make an Institutional Commitment to Online Education. The extent to which a community college commits to distance education will determine the degree to which faculty will support institutional moves to the next stage of technology integration. An institution can demonstrate this commitment through policies, procedures, and rewards that place value on faculty expertise in adapting technology to both the traditional and emerging missions of the community college. However, community colleges must make a sizable investment in professional development if faculty are to move successfully to the next phase of technology integration. Institutions must assist faculty in making the technological and psychological leaps necessary to actively incorporate technology in their teaching and learning processes, and help them adjust to the roles they will play in this online environment.

Setting the Stage for the Next Phase

To meet the challenges of the next phase in online education, community colleges will have to engage in a serious and multifaceted technology audit in order to customize technology to students' needs. They must also create internal and external partnerships to serve the unique needs of community college learners both on campus and at a distance. In addition, community colleges need to enlist external agencies and organizations to help them provide students with state-of-the-art technological learning environments. Furthermore, they should explore ways to generate new revenue by marketing their online courses. Finally, community colleges need to demonstrate their institutional commitment to distance education by providing faculty and staff with systematic professional development, so that all campus constituents can use technology to further both the new and the traditional missions of the community college.

References

Bates, A. W., and Poole, G. *Effective Teaching with Technology in Higher Education: Foundations for Success.* San Francisco: Jossey-Bass, 2003.

Biner, P. M., Bink, M. L., Huffman, M. L., and Dean, R. S. "Personality Characteristics Differentiating and Predicting the Achievement of Televised-Course Students and Traditional-Course Students." In L. Foster, B. L. Bower, and L. W. Watson (eds.), *ASHE Reader—Distance Education: Teaching and Learning in Higher Education* (pp. 340–348). Boston: Pearson Custom, 2002.

Doucette, D. "Transforming Teaching and Learning Using Information Technology: A Report from the Field." *Community College Journal,* 1994, 65(2), 18–24.

Jacobs, A. "The Costs of Computer Technology." *Community College Journal,* 1995, 66(2), 34–37.

McKinney, K. *ERIC Digest: Technology in Community Colleges,* 1996. Los Angeles: University of California, ERIC Clearinghouse for Community Colleges. (ED 399 992)

Palloff, R. M., and Pratt, K. "What We Know About Electronic Learning." In L. Foster, B. L. Bower, and L. W. Watson (eds.), *ASHE Reader—Distance Education: Teaching and Learning in Higher Education* (pp. 224–231). Boston: Pearson Custom, 2002a.

Palloff, R. M., and Pratt, K. "Time and Group Size." In L. Foster, B. L. Bower, and L. W. Watson (eds.), *ASHE Reader—Distance Education: Teaching and Learning in Higher Education* (pp. 331–339). Boston: Pearson Custom, 2002b.

Schifter, C. C. "Teaching in the 21st Century." In L. Foster, B. L. Bower, and L. W. Watson (eds.), *ASHE Reader—Distance Education: Teaching and Learning in Higher Education* (pp. 215–233). Boston: Pearson Custom, 2002.

Van Dusen, G. C. "Classroom Learning: Interaction and Interface." In L. Foster, B. L. Bower, and L. W. Watson (eds.), *ASHE Reader—Distance Education: Teaching and Learning in Higher Education* (pp. 242–248). Boston: Pearson Custom, 2002.

Young, J. R. "Will Colleges Miss the Next Big Thing? Technology Budget Cuts Could Hurt Innovation on Campuses, Officials Worry." *Chronicle of Higher Education,* Apr. 23, 2004, 50(33), A35. http://chronicle.com/prm/weekly/v50/i33/33a03501.htm. Accessed Aug. 18, 2004.

LENOAR FOSTER is associate professor of educational leadership and higher education at Washington State University. He has presented nationally and internationally on the topic of distance education.

Based on regional and national perspectives developed by the Southern Regional Education Board (SREB), this chapter examines policy barriers to e-learning and related challenges community colleges must face if they are to create an open marketplace for e-learning.

Policy: The Inconspicuous Barrier to Expanding E-Learning in Community Colleges

Bruce N. Chaloux

The chapters in this volume paint an impressive picture of the continuing development of distance education in the community college. Increasingly in the mainstream over the past decade, e-learning has been established as a central and critical way to serve students. In particular, e-learning helps community colleges move their goal of universal access "from promise to practice" (Web-Based Education Commission, 2000, p. iv).

Online learning has opened doors to higher education for many students otherwise restricted by fixed schedules and geographic obstacles. However, extending access to traditionally underserved citizens, such as working adults and rural populations, will demand a renewed commitment to establishing a ubiquitous and universally accessible network (Bohland, Papadakis, and Worrall, 2000). Despite extraordinary growth in e-learning programs, there are presently many fields in which e-learning courses are not available or programs are not complete. For example, adult literacy instructor training, workforce training such as in manufacturing technology and criminal justice, teacher training, and allied health lack effective online programs. Yet all these areas are central to the community college mission. More funding is needed, both in the form of direct subsidies for start-up costs and in subsidies to encourage institutions to fill such market gaps through online courses.

All but a small percentage of institutions currently offer online education, yet barriers exist to the continuing development and expansion of e-learning (Allen and Seaman, 2003). Chief among these barriers are policies at the federal, state, and institutional levels that create unobtrusive but real impediments to e-learning. Most of these policies were defined and instituted many years ago in order to help students pursue higher education (Mingle and Chaloux, 2002; Voorhees and Lingenfelter, 2003). Written in a different time, for different students, and with different modes of educational delivery in mind, these policies still benefit some students but create barriers for others, particularly e-learners. This chapter examines these policy barriers, their effect on the e-learning movement, and what can be done to change, reduce, or eliminate them.

Policy Barriers to E-Learning

The Southern Regional Education Board (SREB) is a regional compact of sixteen southern states (Alabama, Arkansas, Delaware, Florida, Georgia, Kentucky, Louisiana, Maryland, Mississippi, North Carolina, Oklahoma, South Carolina, Tennessee, Texas, Virginia, and West Virginia). Since its establishment in 1948, SREB has focused on increasing access to higher education in the South, ensuring educational quality, and serving students who have traditionally not been well-served by higher education. SREB has embraced technology and e-learning as ways to ensure access and quality education for all students in the region.

In the mid-1990s, SREB created a regional educational technology cooperative, and in 1997, launched the Electronic Campus, an electronic marketplace of online courses, programs, and services that now offers over nine thousand credit courses in more than four hundred degree programs at roughly three hundred institutions. Early in the development of the Electronic Campus, clear signs of serious policy challenges and barriers started to emerge. To respond to these challenges, SREB created the Distance Learning Policy Laboratory (DLPL) to study policy and to effect change. Working with over one hundred educators, distance learning experts, policymakers, and state leaders, the DLPL outlines policy challenges to distance learning and makes recommendations for addressing them in a series of reports (http://www.sreb.org). Policies in five areas have emerged as serious yet inconspicuous barriers to e-learning, particularly in community colleges: tuition, credit transfer, funding for e-learning, financial aid, and student support services.

Tuition. Higher education has become less affordable over the past few years in the wake of dramatic increases in tuition (Callan, 2002; College Board, 2003). Although tuition increases may be inevitable in times of state budget shortfalls, e-learning courses can be priced effectively if institutions use a market-oriented pricing structure and eliminate pricing based on residency.

Traditional methods of charging higher tuition and fees to out-of-state students are inappropriate, even unworkable, in e-learning. The high cost of out-of-state tuition, for example, may limit competitive marketing and preclude a college's ability to achieve economies of scale in enrollment. Such out-of-date tuition pricing is also a significant barrier to e-learners who can access programs at colleges hundreds or thousands of miles away, yet cannot afford to take advantage of them. Furthermore, when both in-state and out-of-state e-learners use campus resources and instructional support services in the same way, variable rates based on residency do not make sense.

One approach to eliminating unnecessary e-learning barriers based on tuition is an electronic tuition rate policy currently being promoted in SREB states (Mingle and Chaloux, 2002). This policy allows institutions to establish a market-driven tuition rate for electronically delivered courses and programs that is independent of student residency. The potential benefits of this policy are significant for both students and institutions. Students gain access to a greater number of educational programs at lower prices and with reduced need for financial aid. Community colleges benefit from expanded markets, greater revenues and operating efficiency, better utilization of available capacity, and reduced expenses from unnecessary course duplication.

Credit Transfer. E-learning increases the number and availability of courses and programs, making it possible for more students to balance classes with work and family schedules; thus, it helps accomplish the community college's goal of universal access. Distance learners are able to choose from a wide variety of online courses designed to meet their particular learning needs, and many of them take courses at more than one institution at the same time. These multiple-institution students, sometimes called transients or cherry pickers, must navigate each institution's academic and institutional requirements in order to determine whether credit earned at one college will be recognized by another.

As the number of students who take online courses at more than one institution grows, incongruent credit transfer policies will create higher costs and make it more difficult for students to reach their educational goals. The promise of an education via technology is clearly undermined when students are required to repeat courses in order to meet a particular institution's degree requirements (Southern Regional Education Board, 2002a). Therefore, policies easing credit transfer should be adopted. This should first occur at the state level, but state systems of higher education can no longer work in isolation if e-learning is to grow to its full potential. Because e-learning is independent of physical place or state boundaries, new credit transfer policies and principles should also be adopted regionally, nationally, and eventually, internationally.

SREB has proposed a strategy to allow for more congruent credit transfer by establishing a *degree completer entity* in every state. A degree completer entity could be a virtual campus, a single institution, or a group of institutions that uses mutually agreed-upon criteria to integrate various course credits into meaningful, coherent degrees. Each state would identify one or more institutions or consortia to act as degree completers (Southern Regional Education Board, 2002a).

Another proposed strategy is to establish an *electronic regional transfer crosswalk* that would help students to predetermine graduation requirements and assess transferability of courses from one institution to another. This crosswalk could be built on existing state-based articulation agreements and could eventually extend across multiple states and the nation (Southern Regional Education Board, 2002a).

E-Learning Funding. Despite the growth of e-learning, many states and community colleges still treat it as a special budget item and fund it through onetime appropriations. Other states and institutions regularly fund but have yet to establish e-learning, and its accompanying technology infrastructure, as a core budget item. Current funding policies, although appropriate for traditional campus-based programs, fail to provide sufficient support or flexibility for institutions to expand e-learning programs and services (Southern Regional Education Board, 2002b). Traditional methods and standards of cost estimation such as lump-sum appropriations do not usually work well for e-learning; instead, states and community colleges should fund e-learning and associated technology throughout its life cycle. Allocations should incorporate incentives to support the change processes necessary for effective technology utilization and should be clearly correlated with important objectives to ensure accountability.

As with on-campus educational offerings, the primary costs in technology initiatives are not hardware or software but are the human resources or personnel infrastructure associated with faculty and instructional support staff. Funding policies must address these central and significant costs. Community colleges can reduce human resource costs by encouraging greater institutional support for faculty productivity and effectiveness, initiating cooperative activities that achieve both economies of scale and qualitative improvements, implementing team approaches to curriculum development, and encouraging and supporting the creation and effective use of digital learning materials (Southern Regional Education Board, 2002b).

Financial Aid. Although federal and state governments offer billions of dollars in financial aid, little is available to distance learners (Wolff, 2001). Indeed, financial aid mechanisms designed to expand access to higher education often limit aid for students who are not of traditional college age, do not attend full time, or do not enroll in on-campus classes (Carnevale, 2001a, 2001b). These barriers must be removed as soon as possible to allow the fastest-growing population of college students—e-learners—to receive financial aid.

Financial aid systems at all levels should remove or lessen financial barriers and make higher education available to all who can benefit. Thus, financial aid providers must widen their definition of a college student and become more responsive to the different ways, places, and formats in which students learn. To assist in this effort, policymakers should devise strategies to provide greater flexibility for e-learners and financial aid providers. Assessing the practicality, efficiency, and effectiveness of shifting financial aid disbursement from an institution-based to a student-based model is the first step in this process. Community colleges should also promote changes in existing federal financial aid statutes and regulations and should redefine academic learning periods to allow institutions and students to use financial aid for overlapping academic terms, self-paced learning, short and sequential course enrollment, and multiple or rolling start dates. As well, community colleges and policymakers should develop procedures that permit specific e-learning expenses to be included in financial aid calculations (Southern Regional Education Board, 2002c). Finally, SREB advocates the development of a regional financial aid clearinghouse for e-learners. This clearinghouse would facilitate multistate and multi-institutional financial aid policies, and would especially benefit e-learners enrolled in more than one institution at the same time.

Student Support Services. Although community colleges have moved rapidly in the past decade to develop online courses and degree programs, few provide the full array of academic and administrative services necessary to support online learners (Southern Regional Education Board, 2002c; Western Cooperative for Educational Telecommunications, 2001). Policies that ensure e-learners have access to appropriate and adequate support services can be created in a variety of ways. First, community colleges in a particular state or region can collaborate to create economies of scale for online student services. By pooling resources, institutions can reduce costs and program duplication and offer greater depth and breadth of services. Community colleges can also employ learner-centered customer relationship management models to help ensure that instructional activities and support services truly meet student needs (Southern Regional Education Board, 2002c).

As Chapter Seven explains, many services designed for distance learners also serve on-campus students. Therefore, policies are needed to encourage moving traditionally campus-based services such as financial aid, admission and enrollment, registration, library and bookstore services, academic advising, career counseling, and skills testing to the Web. Significant modification may be needed to make some of these services available to e-learners, but the growing use of instructional technology in both on-campus and off-campus education makes these new delivery formats necessary.

Conclusion

E-learning has become a significant strategy in increasing access to higher education. However, community colleges are often hamstrung by myriad state and federal policies and practices that are ineffective or even deny access to e-learners. Community colleges must work to change policies on tuition, credit transfer, funding, financial aid, and student services that hamper access to e-learning. Because community colleges have strong links to local communities, are committed to e-learning, and can be flexible in response to changing market conditions, they can and should take a leadership role in developing better local, regional, and national e-learning policies.

References

Allen, I. E., and Seaman, J. *Sizing the Opportunity: The Quality and Extent of Online Education in the United States, 2002 and 2003.* Needham, Mass.: Sloan Center for Online Education, 2003.

Bohland, J., Papadakis, M., and Worrall, R. *Creating the CyberSouth.* Research Triangle Park, N.C.: Southern Growth Policies Board, 2000.

Callan, P. M. *Coping with Recession: Public Policy, Economic Downturns, and Higher Education.* Washington, D.C.: National Center for Public Policy and Higher Education, 2002.

Carnevale, D. "Report to Congress Says Financial-Aid Rules Are Hurting Distance Programs." *Chronicle of Higher Education,* Jan. 24, 2001a, 47(22), A34. http://chronicle. com/prm/weekly/v47/i22/22a03402.htm. Accessed Aug. 18, 2004.

Carnevale, D. "House Votes to Ease Regulations on Distance Education." *Chronicle of Higher Education,* Oct. 26, 2001b, 48(9), A38. http://chronicle.com/prm/weekly/ v48/i09/09a03803.htm. Accessed Aug. 18, 2004.

College Board. *Trends in College Pricing.* New York: College Board, 2003.

Mingle, J. R., and Chaloux, B. N. "Technology Can Extend Access to Postsecondary Education: An Action Agenda for the South." Atlanta: Southern Regional Education Board, 2002.

Southern Regional Education Board, Distance Learning Policy Laboratory. "Distance Learning and the Transfer of Academic Credit: A Report of the SREB Distance Learning Policy Laboratory Credit Issues Subcommittee." Atlanta: Southern Regional Education Board, 2002a.

Southern Regional Education Board, Distance Learning Policy Laboratory. "Using Finance Policy to Advance Distance Learning: A Report of the SREB Distance Learning Policy Laboratory Finance Subcommittee." Atlanta: Southern Regional Education Board, 2002b.

Southern Regional Education Board, Distance Learning Policy Laboratory. "Creating Financial Aid Programs That Work for Distance Learners: A Report of the SREB Distance Learning Policy Laboratory Financial Aid Subcommittee." Atlanta: Southern Regional Education Board, 2002c.

Voorhees, R. A., and Lingenfelter, P. E. *Adult Learners and State Policy.* Denver: State Higher Education Executive Officers Association and the Council for Adult and Experiential Learning, 2003.

Web-Based Education Commission. "The Power of the Internet for Learning: Moving from Promise to Practice. Report to the President and Congress of the United States." Washington, D.C.: Web-Based Education Commission, 2000. http://www.ed.gov/ offices/AC/WBEC/FinalReport/index.html. Accessed Aug. 18, 2004.

Western Cooperative for Educational Telecommunications. *Guide to Developing Online Student Services.* Boulder, Colo.: Western Interstate Commission for Higher Education, Western Cooperative for Educational Telecommunications, 2001. http://www.wcet. info/resources/publications/guide/guide.htm. Accessed Aug. 18, 2004.

Wolff, P. "Very Part-Time Students Are Hobbled by Very Little Financial Aid." *Chronicle of Higher Education,* Mar. 16, 2001, 47(27), B20. http://chronicle.com/prm/weekly/ v47/i27/27b02001.htm. Accessed Aug. 18, 2004.

BRUCE N. CHALOUX *is director of the Electronic Campus and heads the Distance Learning Policy Laboratory for the Southern Regional Education Board in Atlanta.*

11

This chapter presents additional information and resources for distance educators at community colleges, focusing in particular on the Americans with Disabilities Act, the TEACH Act, and learning objects and models.

Sources and Information for Distance Educators

Veronica Diaz

Community colleges exist in what Meyer (2002) has described as a changing educational marketplace, increasingly global in orientation, where technology enables the delivery of a variety of educational programs. In an era of diminished state and federal funds for institutions of higher education, many community colleges are pursuing technological solutions in order to provide dynamic instruction to an increasingly diverse community college student population, and to improve student learning outcomes.

Despite its benefits, however, there are many challenges in designing and implementing successful distance programs. For instance, students with disabilities may not have access to e-learning opportunities because learning technologies do not always offer products that accommodate them. Distance education also faces new challenges in the form of changing copyright laws. In October 2002, Congress passed the Technology, Education and Copyright Harmonization (TEACH) Act in order to address the lawful uses of copyrighted materials in distance education environments. The TEACH Act raises many questions and challenges for community college distance educators. Community colleges are also constantly challenged by the development and implementation of new distance learning technologies. The use and sharing of learning objects, for example, forces institutions to struggle with quality, standards, maintenance, cataloguing, and control.

This chapter outlines several ERIC documents, informational Web sites, and other resources pertaining to distance learning at community colleges. In particular, it provides additional resources and information about the Americans with Disabilities Act and how it affects distance learning at community colleges; copyright laws and intellectual property, including the new TEACH Act; and the creation, sharing, and use of learning objects and models in community college distance instruction.

Americans with Disabilities Act

Providing access to educational information technology is essential if community colleges are to enable students with disabilities to fully participate in today's high-tech world. Technology helps eliminate some of the barriers previously faced by disabled students, but to be successful in providing these students with access, community colleges must address a range of issues, from physical access to visual impairment. Community colleges must work to make instructional technology and other forms of distributed learning available to students with sensory, mobility, learning, and other disabilities. Although national research assessing the impact of the Americans with Disabilities Act on community college distance learning practices is relatively limited, the resources in this section provide distance educators with information about this important topic.

Oblinger, D., and Ruby, L. *Accessible Technology: Opening Doors for Disabled Students,* n.d. Boulder, Colo.: EDUCAUSE: http://www.educause.edu/ir/library/pdf/CSD3273.pdf
This report from the EDUCAUSE library showcases successful accessibility programs at the University of Washington, the University of Texas-Austin, the University of Wisconsin at Madison, and Rio Salado Community College in Arizona. Although only one of these programs resides at a community college, practitioners at two-year colleges can benefit from the practices and recommendations discussed.

Disability Resources on the Net: http://www.disabilityresources.org/DISTANCEED.html
Disability Resources, Inc., a nonprofit organization established to promote awareness, availability, and accessibility of information to help people with disabilities, devotes a special section on its Web site to disability resources for distance education. The site monitors and provides links to hundreds of publications, audiovisual materials, and other online resources. Disability Resources, Inc., also reviews and reports on worthwhile materials in its *Disability Resources Monthly* newsletter (http://www.disabilityresources.org/DRMpubs-DRM.html).

Equal Access to Software and Information (EASI): http://www.rit.edu/~easi/index.htm
EASI is an independent, nonprofit 501(c)(3) organization offering excellent information and guidance to community colleges seeking to provide access to instructional technologies for individuals with disabilities.

EASI informs colleges, universities, K–12 schools, and libraries about developments and advancements in the adaptive computer technology field. The EASI Web site offers information on accessibility training and serves as a rich source of information on e-learning accessibility issues.

National Center on Accessible Information Technology in Education (AccessIT): http://www.washington.edu/accessit/index.php
   Funded by the U.S. Department of Education's National Institute on Disability and Rehabilitation Research, the National Center on Accessible Information Technology in Education (AccessIT) works to increase access to information technology for individuals with disabilities. AccessIT develops and disseminates materials, training programs, and technical assistance that facilitate adoption of policies and practices to increase use of accessible information technology. AccessIT's Web site provides a complete list of promising practices and showcases examples of accessible educational information technology.

Title Five Regulations on Distance Education: http://www.curriculum.cc.ca. us/Curriculum/RegulationsGuidelines/Regulations_DistanceEd.htm
   Title Five of the California Education Code governs community college curriculum and matriculation regulations. In July 2002, final Title Five regulations were adopted for distance education. This site contains guidelines for following distance education requirements imposed by the Americans with Disabilities Act. Community college educators might also examine *Guidelines for Good Practice: Effective Instructor-Student Contact in Distance Learning* (http://www.curriculum.cc.ca.us/Curriculum/ GoodPract/ EffectiveInstructor_Student.htm) and *Guidelines for Good Practice: Technology-Mediated Instruction* (http://www.curriculum.cc.ca.us/Curriculum/ GoodPract/tech_mediated_instruction.htm).

Copyright Legislation

The increased use of e-learning in higher education has had profound implications on intellectual property policy. In addition, advances in instructional technology, as well as the legal changes incorporated into the Digital Millennium Copyright Act, have focused concern on the issue of intellectual property. In order to address this issue, Congress enacted the Technology, Education and Copyright Harmonization (TEACH) Act in October 2002. The TEACH Act revised Section 110(2) of the U.S. Copyright Act governing the lawful uses of existing copyrighted materials in distance education, and through specific requirements and conditions, outlines the terms for clipping pieces of text, images, sound, and other works into distance learning activities. As Crews (2002) noted, the TEACH Act is a clear sign that Congress recognizes the importance of distance education, the significance of digital media, and the need to resolve copyright disagreements.

The TEACH Act has many implications for copyright and intellectual property policy in community colleges. Because of the act, institutions must impose restrictions on access, develop new policies, and disseminate copyright information when engaging in distance education initiatives. In addition, many of the act's provisions focus entirely on the behavior of educational institutions rather than on the actions of instructors. Consequently, community colleges, rather than the instructors themselves, take on the risk of infringement liability. This creates an incentive for institutions to become more involved in overseeing educational programs and in selecting and using educational materials. As Crews (2002, p. 3) noted: "The pursuit and regulation of distance education programs will become increasingly centralized within our educational institutions. Because the law calls for institutional policymaking, implementation of technological systems, and meaningful distribution of copyright information, colleges and universities may well require that all programs be transmitted solely on centralized systems that meet the prescribed standard."

The following resources and information provide community college distance educators with guidelines and recommendations for copyright implementation. Several of the Web sites contain current information and best practices that can be useful in ensuring compliance.

Chang, V. *Policy Development for Distance Education. ERIC Digest.* Los Angeles: University of California, ERIC Clearinghouse for Community Colleges, 1998. (ED 423 922)

This ERIC digest, drawn from the New Directions for Community Colleges volume titled *Building a Working Policy for Distance Education,* discusses key policy issues faced by community colleges and other institutions of higher education involved in distance learning. It argues that existing educational practices cannot accommodate distance education without making organizational changes in teaching and learning, as well as in state, federal, and institutional policies. The digest further argues that distance education is more likely to be adopted if it is perceived to be compatible with the college's mission and is effective from both academic and cost perspectives.

Salamon, K. D., and Goldstein, M. B. "Copyright Issues and Technology-Mediated Instruction." In R. C. Cloud (ed.), *Legal Issues in the Community College.* New Directions for Community Colleges, no. 125. San Francisco: Jossey-Bass, 2004.

This chapter gives an overview of intellectual property and copyright law pertaining to telecommunicated instruction. Taking a legal perspective, the chapter reviews issues in changing federal law and related policy, and examines emerging trends in instructional and intellectual property policies.

American Library Association: Distance Education and the TEACH Act: http://www.ala.org/ala/washoff/WOissues/copyrightb/distanceed/distanceeducation.htm

The American Library Association has historically been at the forefront of copyright issues. This site contains one of the best and most comprehensive discussions of the TEACH Act's legislative history, and thoroughly explains the implications of the new copyright law for distance education. Additional higher education copyright resources and links also are provided.

North Carolina State University: The TEACH Toolkit: http://www.lib.ncsu.edu/scc/legislative/teachkit

North Carolina State University (NCSU) has developed a TEACH toolkit that contains an overview of specific TEACH Act requirements, a TEACH glossary, the actual text of the TEACH Act, and a report by the Senate Committee on the Judiciary. The site also contains specific guidelines for distance education practitioners, a detailed checklist for institutions, and a sample NCSU copyright permissions guide with several sample forms. A best practices area includes authentication and digitization guidelines. Finally, the site posts a discussion about the interaction between the TEACH Act and fair use policies, as well as a comprehensive frequently asked questions section addressing institutional-level, technological, faculty, and content questions.

Pima Community College: Copyright and the TEACH Act: http://www.library.pima.edu/copyright.htm

Pima Community College District (Arizona), one of the largest in the country, has developed a comprehensive Web site that details how the district's policies address the TEACH Act's requirements. Links are also provided to other current higher education copyright resources. This is an especially useful site for community college administrators looking to model their policies after a large community college that is active in various forms of distance education.

Learning Objects and Models

A learning object is any digital asset that is used to achieve a learning objective and can be reused in different contexts. Learning objects may be data or data sets, text, images or image collections, audio or video materials, executable programs, courses offered through course management systems, or other resources that can be delivered electronically. Most agree that learning objects should be reusable over time and location, and operable across different systems and software.

Learning objects have the potential to provide individualized learning experiences adapted to students' learning styles, prior knowledge, and specific learning needs. They may also offer great value, saving time and money in course development, increasing the reusability of content, enhancing students' learning environments, sharing knowledge in and across disciplines, and engaging faculty in a dynamic community of practice (Bennett, Diaz, McArthur, and Metros, 2002). The following resources provide community college distance educators with information about creating, sharing, and using learning objects and models.

Bratina, T., Hayes, D., and Blumsack, S. "Preparing Teachers to Use Learning Objects." *Technology Source,* Nov.-Dec. 2002. http://ts.mivu.org/default. asp?show=article&id=961

This paper describes the advantages of using learning objects in technology-supported instruction and is a useful resource for community college educators who are in the early stages of implementing and using learning objects. It discusses reasons why instructors want to implement learning objects and explains how to facilitate their use. Further, it advocates for the effective implementation of existing learning objects, rather than the design of new objects.

National Learning Infrastructure Initiative, Learning Objects. "The Digital Repository Comes of Age: How NLII Members Are Turning Learning Objects into Knowledge Agents." *NLII Annual Review, The New Academy,* 2003: http://www.educause.edu/nlii/annual_review/2003/thedigital repository.asp

This National Learning Infrastructure Initiative (NLII) paper provides a good overview of learning objects and introduces a broader context for their application. It also identifies key institutions and agencies involved in the use of learning objects and learning object models, and provides numerous resources on the subject. Community college practitioners can use this site as an introduction to learning object issues, and can connect themselves to other institutions and individuals active in their application.

National Learning Infrastructure Initiative: Learning Objects: http://www. educause.edu/nlii/keythemes/2004/lo.asp

NLII's learning object Web site outlines the organization, management, and accessibility of learning object repositories, the ways learning objects can enable faculty to develop more effective learning environments, the standards and technical specifications for developing learning objects, cost and benefit information, and policy issues related to learning objects, such as intellectual property and copyright. This site is also a rich source of information about current literature and research on learning objects.

New Media Consortium: Learning Object Initiative: http://www.nmc. org/projects/lo/index.shtml

The New Media Consortium, an international, nonprofit consortium of nearly two hundred leading colleges, universities, and museums, serves as a mechanism for the development of new technology applications that support teaching and learning. It also sponsors programs and activities designed to stimulate innovation. The Learning Object Initiative seeks to detail the theories, standards, projects, tool sets, and repositories for learning objects, to highlight and recognize successful models for developing and deploying learning objects, and to support the further development of learning objects and repositories in higher education.

References

Bennett, K., Diaz, V. M., McArthur, D., and Metros, S. "The Promise and Pitfalls of Learning Objects: Current Status of Digital Resource Collections." Paper presented at the National Learning Infrastructure Initiative Focus Session, San Diego, 2002. http://www.educause.edu/asp/doclib/abstract.asp?ID=NLI0201. Accessed July 29, 2004.

Crews, K. D. "New Copyright Law for Distance Education: The Meaning and Importance of the TEACH Act," 2002. http://www.ala.org/ala/washoff/WOissues/copyrightb/distanceed/teachsummary.pdf. Accessed Aug. 19, 2004.

Meyer, K. *Quality in Distance Education: Focus on Online Learning.* ASHE-ERIC Higher Education Report, vol. 29, no. 4. San Francisco: Jossey-Bass, 2002.

VERONICA DIAZ is the learning technologies manager for the Eller College of Management and also works with the Learning Technologies Center at the University of Arizona.

INDEX

Access and technology, 31–37, 75
Agassiz, C., 6
Albright, M., 6, 7, 47
Allen, I. E., 79
Americans with Disabilities Act, 86–87
Andrews, C. R., 2, 65, 72
Armitage, S., 57
Arreola, R. A., 47
Assessment methods, 51
Asynchronous activities, 8, 50
Atkins, D. E., 28

Baker, W. J., 8
Barnard, J., 8
Barone, C. A., 26, 28
Barr, R., 51
Bates, A. W., 74, 75, 76
Beaudoin, M. F., 28
Bennett, K., 89
Berge, Z. L., 26
Bergmann, H. F., 6
Biner, P. M., 75
Bink, M. L., 75
Blumsack, S., 90
Boccuti, C., 25
Bohland, J., 79
Bothun, G. D., 9
Bower, B., 1, 2, 3, 5, 12, 47, 54
Bratina, T., 90
Bruso, J. L., 55

Callan, P. M., 80
Carnevale, D., 35, 82
Casey-Powell, D., 2, 55, 64
Challenges in distance education, 10–11, 73–78. See also Policy barriers
Chaloux, B. N., 3, 79, 80, 81, 84
Chang, V., 88
Cleveland, E., 6
Compora, D. P., 25
Copyright issues, 52, 87–89
Costs of e-learning, 19, 39–45, 74–75
Course development: content organization, 49–50; cost of, 42; hybrid courses, 75–76
Course ownership, 52. See also Copyright issues
Cox, D. H., 58

Credit transfer, 81–82
Crews, K. D., 52, 87, 88

Dalziel, C., 63
Dean, R. S., 75
Demographics and Internet access, 33
Desjardins, C., 36
Diaz, V., 3, 85, 89, 91
Dillon, C. L., 48
Dirr, P. J., 56
Distance education: challenges in, 10–11, 73–78; in community college, 8–10; conclusions on, 11; defined, 5; history of, 6–8. See also Successful programs
Doucette, D., 9, 74
Duderstadt, J. J., 28
Duin, A. H., 26

Extended Learning Institute (ELI), 23–29

Faculty: role of, 48, 75; training for, 16, 41–42; workload of, 48–49
Fetherston, T., 10, 47, 51
Financial aid, 82–83
Fleit, L. H., 37
Floyd, D. L., 2, 55, 57, 64
Foster, L., 3, 73, 78
Foster, T. J., 7

Gallagher, P. J., 25
Gilbert, S., 36
Gillespie, F., 48
Gladieux, L. E., 36
Gloster, A. S., 8
Goldstein, M. B., 88
Graham, C., 50
Gross, D., 25, 28
Gross, R., 25, 28

Hardy, K., 1, 2, 3, 5, 12, 47, 54
Harper, W. R., 7
Hartman, J. L., 26, 27
Hawkins, B. L., 26, 27, 28
Hayes, D., 90
Helfgot, S. R., 55
Heterick, R. C., 26

History of distance education, 6–8
Hitt, J. C., 26, 27
Hoffman, R., 49
Holmberg, B., 6, 7
Howell, S. L., 14
Huffman, M. L., 75
Hybrid courses, 75–76

Inman, E., 8
Intellectual property issues, 52, 87–89

Jacobs, A., 74
Johnson, J. L., 15
Johnstone, S., 9, 41, 42
Jones, D., 40

Kerwin, M., 8
Kruse, K., 42

LaMonica, L., 47, 49, 50
Langenscheidt, G., 6
Leach, E., 9
Learning Anytime Anyplace Partnership
    (LAAP), 57
Learning objects and models, 89–91
Levine, A., 28
Levine, T. K., 25
Levy, S., 25, 26, 28
Light, J. S., 31
Lindsay, N. K., 14
Lingenfelter, P. E., 80
Lynch, M. M., 15, 50

Madden, M., 33
Matthews, D., 31
Mayes, L., 8
McArthur, D., 89
McKinney, K., 74
McPhail, I. P., 9
Menges, R., 47
Metros, S., 89
Meyer, K. A., 17, 85
Meyer, T. T., 25
Miller, T., 58
Mingle, J. R., 26, 80, 81
Mission, institutional, 13–14, 74–75
Moore, P. L., 31
Morgan, B. M., 19
Muilenburg, L., 26

O'Banion, T., 25, 48, 51
Oblinger, D. G., 26, 28, 36, 86

Olcott, D., Jr., 49
Oliver, R., 47, 49
Olliver, J., 1, 13, 21
Oregon's distance learning consortium,
    65–72

Palloff, R. M., 75
Papadakis, M., 79
Payne, M., 63
Phillipps, C., 6
Pirkl, R., 25, 28
Pitman, I., 6
Policy barriers, 79–83
Poole, G., 74, 75, 76
Poulin, R., 41, 42
Pratt, K., 75
Prince, J., 58

Ruby, L., 86
Rush, S. C., 34, 36
Ryland, J. N., 34

Sachs, S. G., 2, 23, 24, 26, 27
Salamon, K. D., 88
Scarafiotti, C., 2, 39, 46
Schifter, C. C., 75
Seaman, J., 79
Seaman, E., 56
Shea, P., 57
Simonson, M., 6, 7, 47
Smaldino, S., 6, 7, 47
Spector, P., 17
Student support services, 55–63, 83
Successful programs: and accountability,
    19; cost of, 19, 39–45, 74–75; and
    electronic services, 17; existing sys-
    tems for, 20; and faculty training, 16;
    and institutional commitment, 14, 77;
    and institutional mission, 13–14,
    74–75; and market research, 18; and
    pedagogical differences, 14–15; and
    rapid change, 20; and single point of
    contact, 16–17; support networks for,
    17–18
Sun, J. C., 28
Swail, W. S., 36
Synchronous activities, 8, 50

Tagg, J., 51
Tapscott, D., 33
Teaching: and assessment methods, 51;
    role, 48, 75

Technology audits, 76
Technology Costing Methodology, 40
Technology, Education and Copyright
    Harmonization (TEACH) Act, 52, 85,
    86, 87–89
Technology help desk, 41
Ticknor, A. E., 6
Tilson, S., 9
Toussaint, C., 6
Twigg, C. A., 14, 26, 43, 44

Van Dusen, G. C., 75
Van Houweling, D., 28
Voorhees, R. A., 80
Walsh, S. M., 48

Ward, D., 27
Watson, L. W., 2, 31, 38
Weihe, L., 57
Wenger, G. E., 34
Williams, P. B., 14
Wolff, P., 82
Workload, faculty, 48–49
Worrall, R., 79
Wright, S. J., 49

Young, J. R., 74

Zukas, A., 48
Zvacek, S., 6, 7, 47

Back Issue/Subscription Order Form

Copy or detach and send to:
Jossey-Bass, A Wiley Imprint, 989 Market Street, San Francisco CA 94103-1741

Call or fax toll-free: Phone 888-378-2537 6:30AM – 3PM PST; Fax 888-481-2665

Back Issues: Please send me the following issues at $29 each
(Important: please include ISBN number with your order.)

_____

_____

_____

$ _____   Total for single issues

$ _____   SHIPPING CHARGES: SURFACE   Domestic Canadian
                                        First Item $5.00 $6.00
                                        Each Add'l Item $3.00 $1.50
                        For next-day and second-day delivery rates, call the number listed above.

Subscriptions   Please __ start __ renew my subscription to *New Directions for Community Colleges* for the year 2____ at the following rate:

U.S.	__ Individual $80	__ Institutional $165
Canada	__ Individual $80	__ Institutional $165
All Others	__ Individual $104	__ Institutional $239
Online Subscription		__ Institutional $165

**For more information about online subscriptions visit
www.interscience.wiley.com**

$ _____   Total single issues and subscriptions (Add appropriate sales tax for your state for single issue orders. No sales tax for U.S. subscriptions. Canadian residents, add GST for subscriptions and single issues.)

__Payment enclosed (U.S. check or money order only)
__VISA __ MC __ AmEx __ # _____Exp. Date _____

Signature _____ Day Phone _____
__ Bill Me (U.S. institutional orders only. Purchase order required.)

Purchase order # _____
               Federal Tax ID13559302   **GST 89102 8052**

Name _____

Address _____

_____

Phone _____ E-mail _____

For more information about Jossey-Bass, visit our Web site at www.josseybass.com

OTHER TITLES AVAILABLE IN THE
NEW DIRECTIONS FOR COMMUNITY COLLEGES SERIES
Arthur M. Cohen, Editor-in-Chief
Florence B. Brawer, Associate Editor

CC127   **Serving Minority Populations**
Berta Vigil Laden
Focuses on how colleges with emerging majority enrollments of African
American, Hispanic, American Indian, Asian American and Pacific Islander,
and other ethnically diverse students are responding to the needs—
academic, financial, and cultural—of their increasingly diverse student
populations. Discusses partnerships with universities, businesses,
foundations, and professional associations that can increase access,
retention, and overall academic success for students of color. Covers best
practices from Minority-Serving Institutions, and offers examples for
mainstream community colleges.
ISBN: 0-7879-7790-X

CC126   **Developing and Implementing Assessment of Student Learning Outcomes**
Andreea M. Serban, Jack Friedlander
Colleges are under increasing pressure to produce evidence of student
learning, but most assessment research focuses on four-year colleges. This
volume is designed for practitioners looking for models that community
colleges can apply to measuring student learning outcomes at the classroom,
course, program, and institutional levels to satisfy legislative and
accreditation requirements.
ISBN: 0-7879-7687-3

CC125   **Legal Issues in the Community College**
Robert C. Cloud
Community colleges must be prepared for lawsuits, federal statutes, court
rulings, union negotiations, and other legal issues that could affect
institutional stability and effectiveness. This volume provides leaders with
information about board relations, tenure and employment, student rights
and safety, disability law, risk management, copyright and technology
issues, and more.
ISBN: 0-7879-7482-X

CC124   **Successful Approaches to Fundraising and Development**
Mark David Milliron, Gerardo E. de los Santos, Boo Browning
This volume outlines how community colleges can tap into financial support
from the private sector, as four-year institutions have been doing. Chapter
authors discuss building community college foundations, cultivating
relationships with the local community, generating new sources of revenue,
fundraising from alumni, and the roles of boards, presidents, and trustees.
ISBN: 0-7879-7283-5

CC123   **Help Wanted: Preparing Community College Leaders in a New Century**
William E. Piland, David B. Wolf
This issue brings together various thoughtful perspectives on the nature of
leading community colleges over the foreseeable future. Authors offer
suggestions for specific programmatic actions that community colleges
themselves can take to provide the quantity, quality, specializations, and
diversity of leaders that are needed.
ISBN: 0-7879-7248-7

NEW DIRECTIONS FOR COMMUNITY COLLEGES IS NOW AVAILABLE ONLINE AT WILEY INTERSCIENCE

What is Wiley InterScience?

Wiley InterScience is the dynamic online content service from John Wiley & Sons delivering the full text of over 300 leading scientific, technical, medical, and professional journals, plus major reference works, the acclaimed *Current Protocols* laboratory manuals, and even the full text of select Wiley print books online.

What are some special features of Wiley InterScience?

Wiley InterScience Alerts is a service that delivers table of contents via e-mail for any journal available on Wiley InterScience as soon as a new issue is published online.
Early View is Wiley's exclusive service presenting individual articles online as soon as they are ready, even before the release of the compiled print issue. These articles are complete, peer-reviewed, and citable.
CrossRef is the innovative multi-publisher reference linking system enabling readers to move seamlessly from a reference in a journal article to the cited publication, typically located on a different server and published by a different publisher.

How can I access Wiley InterScience?

Visit http://www.interscience.wiley.com

Guest Users can browse Wiley InterScience for unrestricted access to journal Tables of Contents and Article Abstracts, or use the powerful search engine.
Registered Users are provided with a *Personal Home Page* to store and manage customized alerts, searches, and links to favorite journals and articles. Additionally, Registered Users can view free Online Sample Issues and preview selected material from major reference works.
Licensed Customers are entitled to access full-text journal articles in PDF, with select journals also offering full-text HTML.

How do I become an Authorized User?

Authorized Users are individuals authorized by a paying Customer to have access to the journals in Wiley InterScience. For example, a university that subscribes to Wiley journals is considered to be the Customer. Faculty, staff and students authorized by the university to have access to those journals in Wiley InterScience are Authorized Users. Users should contact their Library for information on which Wiley journals they have access to in Wiley InterScience.

ASK YOUR INSTITUTION ABOUT WILEY INTERSCIENCE TODAY!

United States Postal Service

Statement of Ownership, Management, and Circulation

1. Publication Title	2. Publication Number	3. Filing Date
New Directions For Community Colleges	0 1 9 4 - 3 0 8 1	10/1/04

4. Issue Frequency	5. Number of Issues Published Annually	6. Annual Subscription Price
Quarterly	4	$170.00

7. Complete Mailing Address of Known Office of Publication (Not printer) (Street, city, county, state, and ZIP+4)

Wiley Subscription Services, Inc. at Jossey-Bass, 989 Market Street, San Francisco, CA 94103

Contact Person
Joe Schuman

Telephone
(415) 782-3232

8. Complete Mailing Address of Headquarters or General Business Office of Publisher (Not printer)

Wiley Subscription Services, Inc. 111 River Street, Hoboken, NJ 07030

9. Full Names and Complete Mailing Addresses of Publisher, Editor, and Managing Editor (Do not leave blank)

Publisher (Name and complete mailing address)

Wiley, San Francisco, 989 Market Street, San Francisco, CA 94103-1741

Editor (Name and complete mailing address)

Arthur M. Cohen, Eric Clearinghouse for Community Colleges, 3051 Moore Hall, Box 95121, Los Angeles, CA 90095-1521

Managing Editor (Name and complete mailing address)

None

10. Owner (Do not leave blank. If the publication is owned by a corporation, give the name and address of the corporation immediately followed by the names and addresses of all stockholders owning or holding 1 percent or more of the total amount of stock. If not owned by a corporation, give the names and addresses of the individual owners. If owned by a partnership or other unincorporated firm, give its name and address as well as those of each individual owner. If the publication is published by a nonprofit organization, give its name and address.)

Full Name	Complete Mailing Address
Wiley Subscription Services, Inc.	111 River Street, Hoboken, NJ 07030
(see attached list)	

11. Known Bondholders, Mortgagees, and Other Security Holders Owning or Holding 1 Percent or More of Total Amount of Bonds, Mortgages, or Other Securities. If none, check box → ☑ None

Full Name	Complete Mailing Address
None	None

12. Tax Status (For completion by nonprofit organizations authorized to mail at nonprofit rates) (Check one)
The purpose, function, and nonprofit status of this organization and the exempt status for federal income tax purposes:
☐ Has Not Changed During Preceding 12 Months
☐ Has Changed During Preceding 12 Months (Publisher must submit explanation of change with this statement)

PS Form 3526, October 1999   (See Instructions on Reverse)

13. Publication Title	14. Issue Date for Circulation Data Below
New Directions For Community Colleges	Summer 2004

15.	Extent and Nature of Circulation		Average No. Copies Each Issue During Preceding 12 Months	No. Copies of Single Issue Published Nearest to Filing Date
a.	Total Number of Copies (Net press run)		1681	1741
b. Paid and/or Requested Circulation	(1)	Paid/Requested Outside-County Mail Subscriptions Stated on Form 3541. (Include advertiser's proof and exchange copies)	729	736
	(2)	Paid In-County Subscriptions Stated on Form 3541 (Include advertiser's proof and exchange copies)	0	0
	(3)	Sales Through Dealers and Carriers, Street Vendors, Counter Sales, and Other Non-USPS Paid Distribution	0	0
	(4)	Other Classes Mailed Through the USPS	0	0
c.	Total Paid and/or Requested Circulation (Sum of 15b. (1), (2),(3),and (4)) ▶		729	736
d. Free Distribution by Mail (Samples, compliment-ary, and other free)	(1)	Outside-County as Stated on Form 3541	0	0
	(2)	In-County as Stated on Form 3541	0	0
	(3)	Other Classes Mailed Through the USPS	0	0
e.	Free Distribution Outside the Mail (Carriers or other means)		151	148
f.	Total Free Distribution (Sum of 15d. and 15e.) ▶		151	148
g.	Total Distribution (Sum of 15c. and 15f) ▶		880	884
h.	Copies not Distributed		801	857
i.	Total (Sum of 15g. and h.) ▶		1681	1741
j.	Percent Paid and/or Requested Circulation (15c. divided by 15g. times 100)		82%	83%

16. Publication of Statement of Ownership
☑ Publication required. Will be printed in the ___Winter 2004___ issue of this publication.   ☐ Publication not required.

17. Signature and Title of Editor, Publisher, Business Manager, or Owner

Susan E. Lewis, VP & Publisher - Periodicals

Date 10/01/04

I certify that all information furnished on this form is true and complete. I understand that anyone who furnishes false or misleading information on this form or who omits material or information requested on the form may be subject to criminal sanctions (including fines and imprisonment) and/or civil sanctions (including civil penalties).

Instructions to Publishers

1. Complete and file one copy of this form with your postmaster annually on or before October 1. Keep a copy of the completed form for your records.

2. In cases where the stockholder or security holder is a trustee, include in items 10 and 11 the name of the person or corporation for whom the trustee is acting. Also include the names and addresses of individuals who are stockholders who own or hold 1 percent or more of the total amount of bonds, mortgages, or other securities of the publishing corporation. In item 11, if none, check the box. Use blank sheets if more space is required.

3. Be sure to furnish all circulation information called for in item 15. Free circulation must be shown in items 15d, e, and f.

4. Item 15h., Copies not Distributed, must include (1) newsstand copies originally stated on Form 3541, and returned to the publisher, (2) estimated returns from news agents, and (3), copies for office use, leftovers, spoiled, and all other copies not distributed.

5. If the publication had Periodicals authorization as a general or requester publication, this Statement of Ownership, Management, and Circulation must be published; it must be printed in any issue in October or, if the publication is not published during October, the first issue printed after October.

6. In item 16, indicate the date of the issue in which this Statement of Ownership will be published.

7. Item 17 must be signed.

Failure to file or publish a statement of ownership may lead to suspension of Periodicals authorization.

PS Form 3526, October 1999 (Reverse)